THE RESUME GUIDE FOR WOMEN OF THE '90s

By Kim Marino

Tangerine Press
Santa Barbara, California

Published by:

Tangerine Press
Post Office Box 92213
Santa Barbara, California 93190-2213
U S A

ISBN 0-9624284-8-5

Cover Design by George Delmerico
Illustrations by Rod Tryon
Edited by Martin Perlman

Distributed to the Trade by The Career Press
62 Beverly Road, Hawthorne, NJ 07507 1-(800)-CAREER-1

INTRODUCTION

We've come a long way, baby, or have we? While we account for 52 percent of the American workforce, certainly an impressive number, women still only earn 66 percent of what men make for the same work in the United States. We want good jobs and we want to be fairly compensated for the work we do. In fact, surveys show that the majority of women do not quit a job to raise a family but more often because they feel frustrated by lack of advancement where they work. Women are looking for job opportunities and job satisfaction, certainly two quite reasonable goals.

Women are moving into fields that were previously the sole domain of men -- from engineering, science, and upper management levels of business to editorial positions on men's magazines, high government office, and medicine. Rewarding careers such as nursing and teaching remain reputable goals but not as the only sources for employment these days. (Sure, we want to be teachers and nurses, but we also want to be the administrators and managers in those professions as well.)

This book is designed to help open the doors that will allow women to find those good, challenging jobs and receive the salary they deserve. Kim Marino, founder of "Just Resumes" in Santa Barbara, has helped a wide range of women (and men) do just that. Her techniques enable you to capture your most valuable assets, to see yourself in a new and exciting way -- to gain that all important interview and to go into that interview feeling positive about yourself.

Why a resume book for women? After all, if a woman is going to compete against men for jobs, shouldn't her resume be "manlike"? Actually, Kim

Marino's no-nonsense approach to resume writing is applicable to anyone seeking a job. And in truth the basic elements of a resume, no matter what your gender, political philosophy or favorite color, are essentially the same. But this book includes a number of strategies and resume pointers that can specifically benefit women. First, all the resumes in this book are samples from actual women resume clients of "Just Resumes," taken from a wide range of careers and experiences. If the book does nothing else, the sheer range and diversity of selections can serve as reinforcement, stimulation and inspiration for other women. These are examples of women who are making it.

Second, in many cases there are certain conditions primarily particular to women. Many of you have been out of the work force for many years when you decide to get back out there and find a job. Others of you are entering the work force for the first time, again, after having been at home (doing what Kim will show you is quite valuable work). And numbers of you are starting out, looking for those first jobs or making a big jump to an entirely new area of work, especially areas not traditionally known for high numbers of women employees. For those of you in these circumstances, she offers direct, concrete methods for putting your best foot forward to get that interview (and that job)!

Remember, a professional resume is your first link between you and the potential employer. After reading this book and following Kim's suggestions, you'll have the ability to write your entire resume focused on your career objective. In *The Resume Guide For Women of the '90s*, Kim has included everything you'll need to know to write your own professional resume. She's confident you'll find this book one of the best investments you'll ever make.

ABOUT THE AUTHOR

The founder of "Just Resumes" in Santa Barbara, California, Kim Marino is the author of the highly successful *The College Student's Resume Guide*. She received her practical experience by being out there in the field, going on interviews and finding out what's taking place in the business world. She learned what the employer is really looking for in a potential employee, essentially, what it takes to obtain an interview and what impresses the employer in the interview.

After spending 20 years working for other employers including three years researching the resume market and perfecting her writing style, she started her resume writing service. Personnel agencies, career counselors and a diverse range of clients were quick to recognize the quality of her work. Her referrals now extend throughout the nation and include women and men, professionals in dozens of fields, prominent members of business, industry and government as well as hundreds of college students. Scores of people have written to Kim thanking her for the resumes that have demonstratively improved their lives, and "Just Resumes" has become known as the number one resume writing service to hundreds of satisfied customers.

ACKNOWLEDGEMENT

I would like to give special thanks to the many loyal clients of "Just Resumes" and all the people who offered personal advice, opinions and aid in helping me put this book together:

George Delmerico the artist who designed the book cover. Rod Tryon, the artist who illustrated the artwork throughout the book. Mark Lewis, the photographer who took my picture for the back cover. Jim Cook, the typographyer who typeset the book cover. Lou Kammerer, for helping me out with his expertise on interviewing and job searching. Kenneth Cole, for offering valuable information on executive search firms for me to add to this book. Helen and Harry Kent, and Freda Perlman for believing in me enough to help me get this book printed. And my wonderful, loving and adorable husband Martin Perlman, freelance writer and former Senior Editor for *The Santa Barbara Independent*, for editing the manuscript and giving me valuable input and moral support. This book was printed by McNaughton & Gunn, Saline, Michigan.

DEDICATION

I'd like to dedicate this book to the memory of Jan Fowler, who was a very special person in my life. Whose resume would be filled with goodness and kindness for all the good things she did for others in our community. Who gave me Bogie, who has become such a big part of my life. Who was there whenever we needed her. Also to Gene Fowler, Jan's husband, for being such a wonderful friend over the past five and a half years.

TABLE OF CONTENTS

INTRODUCTION

ABOUT THE AUTHOR

CHAPTER   **PAGE**

TABLE OF CONTENTS

TABLE OF CONTENTS

VIII   ADDITIONAL RESUME SAMPLES (Continued)

IX   COVER LETTER & THANK YOU LETTER SAMPLES

TABLE OF CONTENTS

Chapter I

WHAT IS A PROFESSIONAL RESUME?

Before Getting Started

To effectively use this book, first read all the text in Chapters I, II and III. Then, review the resume samples to obtain an overall sense of what your resume will look like. You'll use the combination of text, scenarios and samples to guide you. Think about your background and what career you want to focus on. This will determine which format is best suited for you. Your choices are either functional, which focuses on your skills, or chronological. You'll want to capture your strongest qualities. After you've finished your first draft, reread the text, scenarios and samples to serve as your reference guide and to help you polish up what you've written.

What a Professional Resume Can Do For You

Your resume is a custom designed, self-marketing tool tailored to your career objectives. It's the first link between you and the potential employer. A professional resume:

1. Focuses the interviewer's attention on your strongest points!
2. Gives you full credit for all your achievements, whether you were paid or not!
3. Guides the interviewer toward positive things to talk about in you!
4. Most importantly, it lets you see yourself in a more focused and positive manner!

Important Things to Know About the Resume

Resumes should be designed so that the receptionist involved in the resume screening process can look at the resume in a 30-second glance and decide to put it in the "Yes" pile. That's the pile that is reviewed by the interviewer. A resume works most effectively in one or two pages; one page is best, if possible. It's very important to have an objective on your resume, even a general objective. The receptionist screening resumes does not want to take the time to figure out what position you're applying for at the company. Also, you'll look more focused, and in turn, be more desirable for the position.

The two basic types of resume formats are functional and chronological. Functional highlights your skills; chronological is simply written in order by date starting with the most recent position and working backwards. (See scenarios and resume samples, Chapters VII and VIII, for a detailed description.) Most people are familiar with the chronological style, your traditional resume format. The functional and chronological resume should both offer the same basic information. The difference is only in how the information is presented.

The chronological resume is used when all these three points apply:

1. Your entire work history includes skills related to your objective.
2. Each position involves a completely different job description.
3. Your work history is stable.

The advantages of a functional resume format are stated below:

1. If your entire work history includes a wide variety of skills, some of which are unrelated to your career objective, you'll create subsections, highlighting only those skills pertinent to your objective.
2. If you've had several positions with the same job description, you'll only say what you did one time, which saves the reader from having to read it over and over again. (See resume samples, Chapters VII and VIII.)

Why Is the Objective So Important on a Resume?

Here's a true story. A client phoned me one day and said she had had a resume professionally written for her by another resume writer. She was getting responses for the wrong type of job. I discovered that her objective was in a cover letter and not in her resume. She was well qualified for several types of jobs, but was only interested in one. Rewriting her entire resume, I added a job objective and designed a functional resume for her, incorporating subtitles directly related to her objective. In turn, the entire resume focused on her objective and she did receive a positive response from the very same company she'd written to before, this time for the position she wanted. (See Pamela Jacobs resume in Chapter VII.)

In some cases your job title will become your objective. This especially applies to certain professionals such as CPAs, Psychologists, Attorneys and Real Estate Associates. (See resume samples in Chapters VII and VIII.)

About Personal Data and Resumes

As a rule, personal data does not belong on resumes these days. Personnel agencies tell me they've run across too much prejudice from the person screening the resumes. Sounds pretty silly, but the receptionist who has the power to give your resume to the interviewer may not like you Libras or Geminis out there, and the interviewer may never even see your resume. Your age, religion and shoe size are not required to appear on a resume.

Chapter II

WRITING TECHNIQUES MADE SIMPLE

Effective Writing Techniques

In a professional resume a lot can be said concisely and vigorously. One-liners are simple, straight forward and work well for resumes. If you prefer paragraph form that's fine too, though I find one-liners work best. Start each sentence with an action word, such as "assisted" or "organized," describing what you do. (See List of Action Words at the end of this lesson.) It's best not to use the same action word twice within a subsection or job description. Remember, for a functional resume, you will create a subsection. The title of each subsection will depend on what skills you highlight to focus on your career objective. (See resume samples, Chapters VII and VIII.)

REMEMBER, ALWAYS THINK POSITIVELY AND FOCUS
ON YOUR JOB OBJECTIVE!

Basic Questions to Ask Yourself For a Functional Resume

Remember the advantages of a functional resume format as listed below.

If your entire work history includes additional skills not related to your career objective, you'll highlight only those skills pertinent to your objective. A functional resume is selective.

If you've had several positions with the same job description, you'll only say what you did one time, which saves the reader from having to read the same material repeatedly. (See resume samples, Chapters VII and VIII.) A functional resume can convey a great deal of information in a minimum amount of space. Now, follow these instructions:

1. List your NAME, ADDRESS & PHONE NUMBER

2. OBJECTIVE

    What is your current objective? For example: a Publicist position for a Major Marketing firm.

3. PROFILE

    This is optional. Your profile is a brief description or summary of personality traits, and achievements related to the objective that the employer may be looking for in you. What are personality traits?

    FOR EXAMPLE: Ability to comfortably work under highly pressured situations and consistently meet strict deadline schedules. (See resume samples chapters VII & VIII.)

4. EDUCATION

    Degree title? Major, What school, graduating date?

5. PROFESSIONAL EXPERIENCE OR RELATED EXPERIENCE

    Starting with the appropriate action word, describe what you do at your job? (See List of Action Words, at the end of this chapter.)

Remember to include any special achievements directly related to your career objective. Always focus on your strongest points that tie in to your career objective. Look at resume samples and read scenarios for more details.

6. EMPLOYMENT HISTORY

    In this section, list your job title, company name, city, state and date position started/ended in chronological order, starting with the most recent and working backwards. If your job title is nondescript or if you didn't have a job title, that's okay, too; simply use a title that describes what you did. Be consistent and list it in chronological order along with the other positions.

How to Organize the Raw Data in a Functional Resume

Although the Employment History section appears last in a functional resume, you'll gain a better perspective on what you're going to write about by listing your EMPLOYMENT or WORK HISTORY before delving into your experience. What you write about under the PROFESSIONAL EXPERIENCE heading essentially will be a description of your achievements and what you've done, taken directly from the EMPLOYMENT or WORK HISTORY section. Remember, always focus on your career objective.

Brainstorm your ideas. There really is no limit to the categories you can create. Start with an action word describing your experiences. After you've listed your achievements and experiences directly related to your career objective, sort out what you wrote. Then, create the subtitles that fit your descriptions of your career objective.

> FOR EXAMPLE: Let's say you're a Portfolio Manager/Trader. You've probably gained valuable skills in Portfolio Management, Trading, Research Analysis & Evaluation.

Basically what you're doing is highlighting the skills the interviewer will be looking for in you for this position as listed in the example above.

List each experience under the appropriate subheading. Visualize the employer receiving your resume. What is he/she looking for in you? Remember, the purpose of this resume is to get you an interview. You only want to include your achievements and experience related to your career objective.

Basic Questions to Ask Yourself For a Chronological Resume
* DO ALL THESE THREE POINTS APPLY TO YOU? *

1. Your entire employment history shows progress with skills related to your objective.

2. Each position involves a generally different job description.

> FOR EXAMPLE: 1989-present   Vice President/Escrow Dept Manager
> 1980-88   Escrow Officer
> 1979-88   Escrow Assistant
> 1978   Escrow Secretary

3. Your work history is stable.

These rules apply to your standard chronological resume format. Simply follow the instructions below.

1. List your NAME, ADDRESS & PHONE NUMBER

2. OBJECTIVE

    What's your current objective? Make it brief and to the point.

    FOR EXAMPLE: An Electrical Engineering position.

3. PROFILE

    This is a brief description or summary of your skills, personality traits, and achievements related to the objective. What are personality traits?

    FOR EXAMPLE: Let's say you want to be an accountant. The interviewer will look for someone who is detail oriented with the ability to meet strict deadline schedules.

4. EDUCATION

    Degree title? Major, What school, graduating date?

5. PROFESSIONAL EXPERIENCE OR RELATED EXPERIENCE

What DATE did you start your present job? (year starting/ending). What's the COMPANY (NAME, CITY and STATE) you presently work for? Describe what you did at each job. Include any special achievements you've accomplished, related to your objective. Always focus on your strongest points, directly related to your career objective. Look at resume samples and read scenarios for more details. Be consistent and repeat the above questions under experience for each position pertinent to your objective.

Another Great Chronological Format...

If the following points apply to your background, there is a variation of the chronological format you may wish to use.

1. You have experience directly related to your objective.
2. Each position involves a completely different job description.

FOR EXAMPLE: 1989-present   Hospital Pharmacy Technician

1982-89   Drug Store Pharmacy Technician

3. And, you also have many other jobs you'd like to actually mention, but they are unrelated to your current objective. (See resume samples in Chapters VII & VIII, Karla, Pharmacy Technician and Hanna, Administrative Assistant/Supervisor.)
4. This format works well if you're making a lateral or upward move within the same company.

Simply follow the same instructions for work experience directly related to your objective listed under PROFESSIONAL OR RELATED EXPERIENCE (see number 5, above).

This time you will also create a section for your unrelated jobs titled EMPLOYMENT HISTORY and list them at the end of your resume. List your job title, company name, city, state and date position started/ended for the rest of your jobs in chronological order starting with the most recent and working backwards.

NOTE, if you've had numerous jobs over the years, you don't <u>have</u> to list them all.

Optional Resume Headings

You may list the following skills or activities under the Professional Profile section or create titles for anything that's pertinent to your career objective and is important to you, such as:

> VOLUNTEER WORK
> ACADEMIC ACHIEVEMENTS
> AFFILIATIONS
> SPECIAL SKILLS
> COMPUTER SKILLS
> OTHER PERTINENT INFORMATION
> LANGUAGE SKILLS

See Resume Samples, Chapters VII & VIII for examples.

LIST OF ACTION WORDS

act as	effect	plan
active in	enact	prepare
administer	establish	present
allocate	evaluate	process
analyze	edit	produce
approve	execute	proofread
articulate	examine	promote
assimilate	follow-up	propose
assist	forecast	provide
assure	formulate	perform
augment	forward to	persuaded
balance	generate	recommend
built	guided	repaired
collect	identify	recruit
communicate	implement	report
compute	inform	research
conceptualize	initiate	resolve
consolidate	integrate	review
consult	interface	revise
contribute	install	represent
control	institute	referred
coordinate	interview	schedule
correct	instruct	screen
correspond	launch	secure
counsel	liaison	select
create	locate	set up
coach	lecture	supervise
chair	lead	supply
demonstrate	maintain	specify
design	manage	systematize
determine	monitor	stimulate
develop	mediate	summarize
direct	market	strengthen
distribute	optimize	test
document	organize	train
draft	oversee	tabulate
delegate	operate	upgrade

Chapter III
FUNCTIONAL VERSUS CHRONOLOGICAL

When to Use What

Your particular background and objective will determine which resume style will work best for you.

Each resume consistently offers the same basic information, though there are several different chronological and functional formats. What do they all have in common?

They all have the same basic titles:

- Name, address and phone number
- Career objective
- Professional profile
- Educational information
- Description of experience
- Employment history stating dates of employment, job title and company name, city and state

And please note:

- All sentences start with the appropriate action verb.
- They all focus on the career objective.

WHAT'S THE DIFFERENCE BETWEEN THE
CHRONOLOGICAL & FUNCTIONAL RESUME?

In the standard chronological resume, the experience and employment history is combined. Dates of employment, job title, company name, city and state with description of experience are listed in chronological order starting with the most recent position and working backwards.

The chronological resume works best for <u>Professional Women</u> making an upward or lateral career move when your background applies to the following rules:

1. Your entire work history shows progress with skills directly related to your job objective.
2. Each position involves a completely different job description.
3. You have a stable work history.

OR...

1. If you had jobs directly related to your objective.
2. Each position involves a completely different job description.
3. And, you also have many unrelated jobs that you'd like to mention, but they really are unrelated to your current objective.

WHAT MAKES THE FUNCTIONAL RESUME DIFFERENT
FROM THE CHRONOLOGICAL RESUME?

1. In the functional resume, all the work experience is highlighted with subsections created, pertinent to the job objective.
2. The entire employment history is listed at the bottom of the resume with job title, company name, city and state in chronological order, separate from experience.

The functional resume works best for the following when your background applies to the rules below:

* 1st Time Job Seekers *

* Professional Women Changing Careers *

* Housewives or Moms Re-entering the Job Market *

1. Your entire work history goes beyond the skills and experience related to your objective.

2. You have skills related to your job objective but not necessarily in your employment history.

3. You've had several positions with the same job description.

Chapter IV

HOUSEWIVES & MOMS ENTERING
OR RE-ENTERING THE JOB MARKET
The Functional Resume Format Works Great For You!

One of the concerns women who have been out of the job market for many years have is that they will not be considered experienced enough to survive in the business world. Recent high school and college graduates looking for their first job may feel the same way. Who would want to hire a "housewife" who raised children for the past 20 years? Who would even look at a resume of a high school senior who has never been gainfully employed? Many of you probably came across the section in Chapter II titled "Professional Experience" and shivered when you faced that imposing label.

You know, the section you thought you'd have to leave blank?
Well, never fear, for I've got great ideas for your resumes. If you have no actual work history, simply write about other important things you've spent your valuable time on. Experience is experience, paid or not; it all counts. The resume is where you can give yourself credit for all the time-consuming, everyday chores you've been doing all these years. Such as...

committees you've been on.

school projects you've worked on.

volunteer work you've done.

FOR EXAMPLE: **Treasurer,** Women's Entrepreneurer Club, 1990-91

PTA President, Kittridge Street School, 1989-90

Coach, Women's Basketball, Vista, CA, 1984-86

ANOTHER EXAMPLE: Being on the PTA committee at school for your kids is a voluntary, unpaid position where you've probably gained valuable communication and organizational skills.

Basically what you're doing is describing the communication and organizational skills you've learned. Once you've completed writing about your experiences, create two subtitle sections:

<u>Communication skills</u>

<u>Organization skills</u>

List each experience under the appropriate subheading. Visualize the employer receiving your resume. What is he/she looking for in you? Again, remember, the purpose of this resume is to get you an interview. You only want to include your achievements and experience related to your career objective.

What about helping your husband out with his work at the office or at home?

FOR EXAMPLE: Doing bookkeeping or banking, scheduling travel arrangements or selling a home.

Other experience such as family/time management includes scheduling appointments for your kids or for yourself, chauffering your children off to school and after-school activities and still managing to have dinner ready on time. Meeting tight deadline schedules? I'll say!

Have you ever nursed a family member, helped a friend or family member through a crisis such as alcoholism or drug addiction. That demonstrates strong interpersonal communication skills and the ability to deal with emergency situations, calmly, quickly and efficiently.

All this "hidden" experience shows the valuable skills that you will highlight to your advantage on your resume in a functional format under many possible subtitles...

> People Management
>
> Time Management
>
> Organization
>
> Problem Solving
>
> Finance
>
> Communication
>
> Interpersonal Communication

Of course, some of you have had actual work experience but haven't worked in many years. The functional resume format also works well for you, because you will highlight your skills under experience and simply list your work history at the bottom of the page (see resume samples in Chapters VII & VIII). Now, you wonder, what do you put down for that gap in time when you weren't working in a paid job? Simple!

FOR EXAMPLE: **Home Mgmt, Travel, Studies**, Boise, ID, 1979-90
OR
Home Mgmt, Research, Studies, Lincoln, NE, 1982-90

That explains what you've been doing, where and when. No gaps in these resumes!

Chapter V

PROFESSIONAL WOMEN
CHANGING CAREERS OR MOVING UP

Making a Lateral or Upward Move in the Same Company

The possibilities for women in all areas of the work world have never been so great. Business, management, medicine, academia -- study hard, earn that degree, and charge into the field of your choice! Right? Yes. But what happens when you've moved into that marketing position or that ad rep job, you've gained more valuable experience, and you now want to either advance further up the company's totem pole or you want to slide sideways into a related field. You need a way of clearly showing your progress and your achievements, a resume that will get results. You want a resume that will show your potential employer that what you're doing is a career and not just a job.

More and more corporations are becoming aware that, even in the '90s, some longstanding traditions and stereotypes by male management prevent women from reaching top corporate levels, even though they may have the talent and experience for such positions. If you feel you are not advancing as quickly as you think you deserve to, a professional resume that highlights your work history can offer just the boost you need to present yourself in the best possible light. Keep trying and create the most effective resume you can -- to show them and you just what you have done and can do!

Now, the chronological format works extremely well for you because it shows your progress and charts your course through the work world. Follow the steps in Chapter II under the subheading of Another Great Chronological Format. Also see Scenario #6 and resume sample in Chapter VII for Hanna Sandrini.

Remember to focus your resume on your career objective. To do this you will highlight all the training you received and duties you're responsible for at your current employer. Under Education add any company training you received. This time you'll title your professional experience CURRENT PROFESSIONAL EXPERIENCE. Highlight the company name, job titles and dates of employment. Let's say that the next step up for you is a supervisor position that just became available at the company you are currently working for.

FOR EXAMPLE: **Objective: Staff Supervisor**

Under the Education heading you'll put, as an example:

UC Davis Training & Development Workshops
Personnel Action Forms...Supervisory
Skills Workshop...Communication Skills
for Women...How to Supervise People.

Under the Current Professional Experience heading:

UNIVERSITY OF CALIFORNIA, Davis, 1984-present
Administrative Assistant
Start with the appropriate action word and describe what you do here.

Senior Clerk
Be consistent and describe what you were responsible for here.

Under Previous Employment History list your earlier jobs:
Clerk, Santa Barbara City Schools, 1982-83
Receptionist, The JPL Corporation, 1980-82

Professional Women Changing Careers

For women seeking a career change, the functional resume format works great. Why? Because the functional resume highlights your skills, not just your employment history. You'll find that you have many more options to choose from when deciding what to highlight in your background that will focus on your current job objective.

FOR EXAMPLE: Let's say you currently have a career as tennis instructor and pre-school teacher. But, recently, you and your husband designed, constructed and sold a condominium. You decided you'd like to become a real estate agent and passed the Real Estate Salesman's [sic] Examination. In a functional resume you will emphasize the skills you have that the interviewer would find appropriate for a realtor. Not only do you have strong communication skills from being a teacher; you now also have real estate experience, a dynamic combination for that profession.

Under the heading of Related Experience:

<u>Real Estate Experience</u>

Emphasize your real estate experience here.

<u>Communication Skills</u>

Highlight the communication skills you've gained here.

See Maryann Scenario #4 in Chapter VII for further details.

When you think about it, what often leads to a major career change are the discoveries about yourself that you make upon embarking on a new hobby, taking a class, or, as in the example above, helping a friend or mate in a special project. These are the unexpected turns in life that translate so well into a functional resume.

Chapter VI

FIRST-TIME JOB SEEKERS

The Functional Resume Is For You!

For those of you with no work history, whether you're graduating from high school or college, that's okay; write about...

1. School projects you've worked on, related to your objective, or

2. Committees you've been in (or) a member of, or

3. Volunteer work you've done.

Include any special achievements, directly related to your career objective. Always focus on your strongest points.

FOR EXAMPLE: Let's say you took architectural classes in high school and/or college. You're starting your second year of college and would like to work in an architectural firm. Under Education list the related classes you took, and under Related Experience make up the appropriate subheadings such as...

Under Objective: A position leading to a career in architecture.

Under Education: **BA Degree, Architecture,** 1993
University of Nebraska, Lincoln, NE
Related Courses: Freehand Prospective Drawing
Design Graphics, CAD CAM Designing, Environmental
Design, Architecture 5

Under Related Experience:

<u>Residential Architectural Projects</u>

* Designed a poolhouse on the CAD CAM computer system.

* Developed design and drew a set of plans for a 200-square-foot beachhouse.

* Designed a two-story townhouse with a family room addition.

This method helps to solve the Catch-22 problem in which a company won't hire you unless you have experience and it seems impossible to gain experience unless you get hired.   By pinpointing your projects and volunteer work, you can demonstrate to employers and to yourself that you do have what it takes to obtain that valued first job!

Chapter VII

RESUME SAMPLES & SCENARIOS

About Scenarios and Resume Samples

The following pages in this chapter consist of scenarios with actual resume samples of my women clients. Each scenario explains the background of the client who comes to me for help in writing that all-important resume. The scenario further explains which format works best and why. There is a brief discussion of the procedure used to write each resume, and you'll see the results in the accompanying sample. Read each one carefully. Then, think about your own background, how it applies to the job you're aiming for, and the way it will fit into your resume.

REMEMBER, it's important that you read all the text in Chapters I-III and review the resume samples to give you a complete sense of what you need in order to write an effective resume.

Searching For the Right Career For You

Are you ready to change careers or just entering the job market, but in either case uncertain about what you'd like to do? Look through the want ads in your local newspaper. See what interests you. Another helpful idea is to combine your hobbies with your skills. Also read newspapers, general interest magazines and specialty publications where you'll find periodic articles on job trends and new kinds of employment.

FOR EXAMPLE: Let's say you love athletics and work well with people; maybe you'd like to consider working for a manufacturer of athletic clothing or equipment as a sales or marketing representative. Read Chapter X, Job Searching and

Interviewing for effective job search techniques used to find positions that aren't always advertised.

And believe it or not, friends and family can be an excellent source of job opportunities. Many times someone knows someone who just mentioned to your best friend that there's an opening for the very kind of job you're interested in at a company in town. Or an uncle who works in the field you're entering may be able to recommend a certain manager or owner you could speak with.

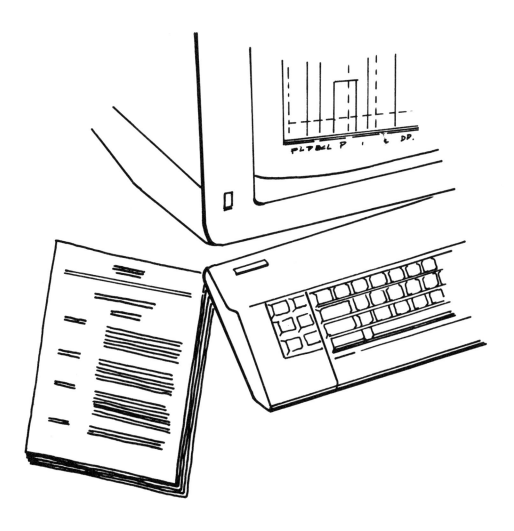

Scenario #1

Pamela, making a lateral career change.

Pamela phoned me one day and said she had had a resume professionally written for her by another resume writer. She was receiving responses but for the wrong type of job. She was the publicity/marketing manager for a highly reputable international broadcasting corporation. She wanted to make the lateral change to product development/marketing manager in the same industry. I discovered that her objective was in a cover letter and not in her resume. Though she was well qualified for several types of jobs, she was only interested in one.

Rewriting her entire resume, I added a job objective and designed a functional resume for her, incorporating subtitles directly related to her objective.

In turn, the entire resume focused on her objective and she did receive a positive response from the very same company she'd written to before, this time for the position she wanted.

PAMELA FENNELL JACOBS
6700 East Valley Road
Los Angeles, CA   90068

(213) 344-9000

OBJECTIVE: A position in Product Development and Marketing Management.

PROFILE:
* Success oriented with high energy and positive attitude.
* Gained valuable personal and business contacts worldwide with thorough product knowledge in the communications and financial news service industries.
* Received extensive financial market and product training, sponsored by Reuters in London, January 1988; FOREX Bourse course, Hong Kong, March 1988.

EDUCATION: BS Degree – Marketing, University of Maryland

QUALIFICATION SUMMARY:

PRODUCT DEVELOPMENT SKILLS
* Promoted new products for Reuters, developed in London and Hong Kong, in the key financial centers of Asia.
* Successfully launched products in all areas of the financial market, working closely with management in 10 countries.
* Developed corporate policy concerning quality, sponsorship, corporate identity, information for shareholders, subsidiary relationships and presented policy to Board of Directors.
* Obtained regulatory approval for direct broadcast of Monitor Service, via VSAT network, in remote Asian countries.
* Successfully streamlined literature and sales training products of Rich Inc, IP Sharp and Finsbury Data Services.
* Designed a 2-year business and quota/commission plan for sales staff.   Generated $4.5M annual sales and $1M first-year profits.
* Developed pricing structures and contracts for all phases of the public radio and satellite service communications industry.
* Developed new business opportunities focusing on private TV and data networks delivered via satellite.

MARKETING MANAGEMENT SKILLS
* Supervised marketing staff and became main source for trouble-shooting among marketing professionals throughout Asia.
* Successfully managed $5M annual budget.
* Managed new product literature including advertising and sales promotion in Asia, Australia and the Middle East.
* Managed all phases of marketing and foreign exchange training programs.   Organized trade shows and major events throughout the Orient, Asia and Australia.

EMPLOYMENT HISTORY:

Marketing Manager Asia, Australia, New Zealand, 1987-88
Reuters Asia Ltd, Hong Kong

Business, Marketing & Planning Manager, 1982-86
National Public Radio, Satellite Services, Washington DC

Scenario #2

Denise, changing careers, functional resume.

Denise came to me when she first started law school. She said she was looking for an entry level, part-time research or writer/editor position in a law office leading to a career in law. She told me she had only had one job over the past 12 years as assistant manager/bookkeeper for a major grocery food chain.

After interviewing Denise, I learned she did have volunteer experience directly related to her job objective. Notice how we added her law-related courses under Education. Beneath the Experience heading we decided to write about her volunteer work under the subheadings of Research Writing & Communication Skills. We added a subheading titled Project Coordination/Management to show her skills in this area as well. Also notice how we simply listed her job of 12 years under Employment History.

This is a great example of a functional resume that works superbly for women with a career change. It's professional and so focused on the job objective, you hardly notice she's changing careers.

DENISE M. CARPENTER
570 Allison Drive
Santa Barbara, CA 93103
(805) 569-1110

OBJECTIVE

Research Assistant, Clerk or Writer/Editor for a Law Firm.

PROFESSIONAL PROFILE

* Developed excellent skills in legal writing and research.
* Highly organized, dedicated with a positive attitude.
* Outstanding ability to communicate with all types of people.
* Work well under pressure; thrive on challenging projects.
* Ranked in the Top 10 of first year students in law school.

EDUCATION

JD, Santa Barbara College of Law
Graduation: 1990   GPA: 3.55

Law-Related Courses

Legal Writing & Research...Criminal Law...Criminal Procedure ...Contracts...Torts...Juvenile Law...Family Law...Wills & Trusts...Personal Property...Real Property...Civil Procedures ...Dispute Resolution...Bioethics

EXPERIENCE

Research Writing & Communication Skills

* Wrote and submitted a client history on behalf of a Cuban detainee at Lompoc Federal Prison.
  - Contacted client's family to verify USA sponsorship.
  - Researched extensive criminal record.
  - Represented and counseled client at an INS deportation hearing.
* Researched and wrote a summary on the origins of Canons of Legal Ethics.
* Participant in a thorough research project to establish a curriculum for the Santa Barbara College of Law Writing and Research class.

Project Coordination/Management

* Prepared income tax returns in conjunction with the IRS and the Volunteer Income Tax Assistance Program.
* Managed a major grocery store in Santa Barbara.
* Hired, trained and supervised 5-100 employees.
* Oversaw the entire budget; responsible for increasing annual profits by 96 percent within the first year.
* Developed and coordinated an effective employee training manual and video.
  - Wrote, directed, casted and introduced the scanner system to 25,000 employees throughout California.

EMPLOYMENT HISTORY

Assistant Mgr/Bookkeeper, Alpha Beta Market, Santa Barbara   1978-present

Scenario #3

Beverly, re-entering the job market, functional resume.

Beverly started acting at the age of five and continued through her high school years. Shortly thereafter she got married, started working in office jobs and raised her children until they were grown.

After attending an actor's workshop sponsored by the 1990 Santa Barbara International Film Festival, she called me up and told me she wanted to get back into acting but hadn't really had any experience for more than 25 years. So we decided to use a functional resume format highlighting all the acting talents she does have. We focused the entire resume on her theatrical experience.

Beverly's resume quickly caught the interest of a casting agent who called from Los Angeles to ask her to come down for an audition.

Beverly's example serves as an inspiration for women who want to re-enter the job market after being out of it for 5, 10, or, even in Beverly's case, 25 years.

BEVERLY A. PERLOFF
Actress

63 Brittany Road
Santa Barbara, CA   93103
(805) 962-6467

Age Range: 40-60
Height/Weight: 5' 5", 165 lbs
Hair/Eyes: Auburn Frosted/Brown

FORMAL ACTOR'S TRAINING

Commercial Workshop, Winter 1990
Jack Rose Agency/Nance Management
Hollywood/Santa Barbara, CA

Professional Acting, W. Hollywood
Players Ring/Players Circle

Professional Acting
Ben Bard Players, W. Hollywood

THEATRICAL EXPERIENCE

Commercial Experience
* "Alphasonics." Played the part of a business person giving a testamonial on the benefits of subliminal tapes aired on four cable TV stations, 1990.

Production/Film Experience
* 60-year old frompy, confused bank robber, "Make It Real," a 10-minute, action/comedy film shown at the closing ceremonies of the 1990 Santa Barbara International Film Festival.
* Team member in writing a script as part of a weekend workshop titled "Make a Movie," sponsored by the 1990 Santa Barbara Int'l Film Festival.
* Wrote, directed and produced original one-act children stage productions.
  - Narrator, story-teller for "The Beginning of the Brownies/Girl Scouts."
* Wrote a 15-minute, one-act comedy for a school production.

Theatre Experience (Elementary-High School)
* Supporting Role-Karen & Inga, "On the Night of January 16th," Fairfax High School, West Hollywood, CA.
* Improv, Cold Reading, One-Act Plays, Scenes, Players Ring & Players Circle, West Hollywood, CA.
* March Hare, "Alice in Wonderland." Los Angeles, CA.
* Supporting Role-Mary, "The Children's Hour." Dramatic three-act play, Los Angeles, CA.
* Assist. Master of Ceremonies, "talent showcase," Los Angeles, CA.
* Tap Dancer, danced "Tea for Two" in a 2-minute talent showcase, 500-seat auditorium, Los Angeles, CA.
* Johnny Ray. Played the part of Johnny Ray's Cry (Lip-sinc), in a exaggerated comedy routine.
* Lead Role, Queen Esther, "Queen of Israel" school production, Los Angeles.
* Created numerous routines for auditions and talent shows.

SPECIAL TALENTS

Scuba diving...golf...tennis...costume design
banker...secretary...photographer...ice skating
model...fashion coordinator.

Scenario #4

Maryann, changing careers, functional resume.

Maryann was receiving her real estate license and wanted to become a real estate agent. She had never professionally worked with real estate before, but she had assisted her husband in the design, construction and sale of their own condominium. So, I created a subheading under Experience and asked her to describe her achievements.

Real Estate agents need to have strong communication and organizational skills. Maryann had sales, promotions and client relation skills from being a tennis instructor. So, I created the appropriate subtitles based on Maryann's background and focused on her objective. I then asked her to describe what her client relations, sales, promotion and organizational skills were. In the Professional Profile, I wrote skills she had to offer based on the needs of a real estate agent. Since Maryann knew she specifically wanted to be a real estate associate, I decided to highlight that in big bold letters, which became her objective.

Notice, under Employment History, I still have her job titles, company names, city, state and dates of employment listed in chronological order. Again, all the basic information written in this functional resume is the same as a chronological resume. The only difference is the way it's presented, in what is emphasized. Also, notice that every line starts with a different action word describing what she did. Once you begin writing in this style, it really becomes quite easy and effective because it's consistent and highlights your skills so well. Maryann's situation is a perfect example of where a functional resume works best to bring out skills and attributes she might never have thought to list. The result is a focused and impressive resume.

MARYANN HOWSER

5001 Kanova Place
Santa Barbara, CA   93103
(805) 569-2220

REAL ESTATE ASSOCIATE

PROFESSIONAL PROFILE

* Experienced in client relations, sales & promotions.
* Organized, dedicated with a positive attitude.
* Outstanding talent for assessing people's needs.
* Proven ability to gain clients' confidence and trust.
* Gained valuable business and personal contacts through-
  out the Santa Barbara community.
* Passed **Real Estate Salesman's Examination**, 1990.

EXPERIENCE

Real Estate Experience
* Assisted in the design, construction & sale of a Santa Barbara condominium.
* Established an effective marketing strategy to promote the sale of property.
  - Designed flyers and newspaper advertising; distributed flyers.
  - Arranged and conducted open house.
* Familiar with blueprints and architectural plans with understanding of conceptual design.

Sales, Promotions & Organization
* Organized and coordinated an entire summer tennis program for children at a private tennis club in Montecito.
* Promoted services through effective telemarketing techniques, thorough product knowledge and exceptional client relations.
* Compiled computer data to keep track of profits & losses of monthly sales.

Client Relations
* Interface with clients and members to interpret their needs and priorities.
* Develop innovative, non-competitive teaching techniques for adults and children, focusing on individual strengths.
* Advise clients and members in a professional and concerned manner, securing their trust and confidence.

EDUCATION & LICENSES

California Real Estate Salesman's License, 1990
BA Degree, Communication, UC Los Angeles, 1979

EMPLOYMENT HISTORY

Tennis Instructor, A Tennis Club, Montecito, CA	1989-present
Teacher's Assistant, Los Angeles School District	1986-88
Pre-School Teacher, Children's Pre-School, Los Angeles, CA	1983-85
Tennis Instructor, City of Los Angeles, Recreation Dept	1978-80

<u>Scenario #5</u>

Julie, making a lateral career change, chronological resume.

Julie's resume demonstrates her progress, step-by-step, from sales associate to assistant manager to store manager. She wanted to use those skills to make a lateral change into a marketing career in the field of banking. We highlighted all her customer relations, cash management and sales ability under the heading of Experience. Also notice how we added a section titled Office Skills to emphasize hidden attributes the interviewer would be looking for in her, skills useful in the banking industry.

Julie got the job at the bank and within six months became their marketing representative.

JULIE MARIE BRIGNELL

5900 Mountain View Road
Seattle, WA   10602
(313) 560-9321

Objective: A Marketing position in the Banking Industry

PROFILE:
* 7-years experience in sales, management and customer relations.
* Highly organized, dedicated with a positive attitude.
* Thrive on working in a challenging environment.
* Excellent written, oral and interpersonal communication skills.
* Problem solver/team player with proven leadership qualities.
* Supervise employees in a professional and tactful manner.
* Born and raised in Seattle, Washington.

EDUCATION:
BA Degree, Communication Studies, 1987
<u>Western Washington University</u>, Bellingham, WA

OFFICE SKILLS:
Light typing...ten key by touch...cash register...daily banking deposits...billing...invoicing...purchasing...quality/inventory control...opening/closing procedures...shipping/receiving...data entry...excellent phone, customer & employee relation skills.

EXPERIENCE:

1987-present
SWEPT AWAY, Seattle, WA
Store Manager/Sales Associate
* Manage entire retail operation at this busy fashion boutique.
* Balance daily cash receipts and handle bank deposits.
* Set up dozens of displays; captured excitement to promote sales.
* Developed a large personal customer base and maintain a preferred customer list that includes customer follow up.
* Maintain opening/closing procedures, shipping/receiving, inventory/quality control, purchasing, pricing, returns and credits.
* Work closely with mfg. representatives to buy merchandise.
* Hire, train, supervise and schedule employees.

1985-87
RAKU, Bellingham, WA
Sales Associate/Assistant Manager
* Assisted manager in all the above at this busy fashion boutique.
* Required excellent customer and employee relations with accurate cash management skills.

Fall/Winter 1985
ARABESQUE, Bellingham, WA
Sales Associate
* Sold clothing and accessories at this fashion boutique on a part-time basis while earning Associate of Arts degree.
* Assisted customers to help them make satisfactory buying decisions while developing a large personal customer base.
* Developed accuracy and speed balancing daily cash transactions.
* Demonstrated strong phone skills, expediting challenges customers presented in a professional manner.

Scenario #6

Hanna, moving up within the same organization, chronological resume.

Hanna's an administrative assistant. Her resume concisely expresses just how much progress she has made within the organization.

Under the Education section, notice that we highlighted how she had received significant additional in-house and company training as well as continuing education on her own.

We then separated the current and previous employment experience to emphasize her positions within the organization. Her job title had been reclassified twice in four years and she still had the same responsibilities. This demonstrates how skilled and ready she was to make a career move up to the position of supervisor. We simply listed her previous employment history just to show the interviewer what other positions she had held in the past.

HANNA SANDRINI
17704 East Valley Road
Irvine, CA 92715
(714) 250-6000

Objective: Administrative Assistant/Supervisor

EDUCATION

* UCI Training & Development Workshops
* Supervision & Communication, Nat'l Seminars
* SB City College: Microsoft Word, WordPerfect
* Advanced Lotus 1-2-3, UCI Extension

UCI Training: Personnel Action Forms...Year-end
Closing (Fiscal)...Supervisory Skills Workshop...
Gen'l Ledger Workshop....Powerful Communication
Skills for Women...How to Supervise People.

CURRENT EMPLOYMENT EXPERIENCE

UNIVERSITY OF CALIFORNIA, Irvine, Physics Accounting Dept. 1984-present
Administrative Assistant II (1987-present)
* Coordinate and implement purchasing and accounting activities.
* Fully responsible for maintaining and executing the recharge system.
* Design and formulate new spreadsheet programs for budget/expense reports and recharge summaries using Lotus 1-2-3 and Excel.
* Track departmental purchases with an account budget of $600K, assuring compliance with University policies/procedures and union contracts.
* Prepare a series of statistical reports from the recharges as well as general and payroll ledgers for the Chairman and MSO.
* Assist administrative staff with payroll.
* Schedule travel arrangements and maintain department files.

Principal Clerk (1986-87)
* Responsible for all the above.

Senior Clerk (1984-86)
* Processed invoices and tracked departmental expenses on a daily basis.

PROFESSIONAL PROFILE

* Gained extensive knowledge of campus administrative policies and procedures through six years of university experience.
* Ability to supervise employees and work with all levels of management in a professional, diplomatic and tactful manner.
* Rapidly analyze/recognize department problems and solutions.
* Work on multiple projects under pressure situations and meet strict deadline schedules and budget requirements.

PREVIOUS EMPLOYMENT HISTORY

Clerk, Irvine City School District	Fall 1983
Public Service/Court Clerk, Municipal Court of Orange County	1979-82
Accounting/Payroll Clerk, The Southland Corporation	1977-79

<u>Scenario #7</u>

Dana, making a career move up the ladder, functional resume.

Dana was a nurse when she came to me for help with a resume. With 20 years nursing experience, she felt it was time she should be hired for the position she had the skills for -- Director of Nursing.

After talking to Dana, I discovered that she had gained all the skills and experience a director of nursing has through the course of her nursing duties. Dana knew she had the experience but had no idea how to bring it out in a resume. By following my techniques for organizing her many experiences and abilities, her resume became the proof of her suitability for the position; it really did come out in her resume quite well. She was skilled in so many areas of nursing, we highlighted those abilities in four subsections under Professional Experience.

Dana is now a Director of Nursing here in Santa Barbara. I was so proud of her when I saw her picture in a press release in the local paper, describing her promotion to one of the top health care agencies in town.

This is another great example of how a really well-written functional style resume can and will make the difference.

DANA E. CLARK

5510 Madison Court
Santa Barbara, CA 93103
(805) 569-1000

Objective: A Director of Nursing position

PROFESSIONAL PROFILE

* 17 years experience in the health care industry.
* Highly skilled in dealing with sensitive populations in a professional and concerned manner.
* Highly organized, dedicated with a positive mental attitude.
* Outstanding written, oral and bilingual communication skills.
* Co-authored an article with Joan Probert, RN, published in the Journal of Christian Nursing, Winter 1985.
* Member, National Hospice Nurses Association and Nurses Christian Fellowship.
* Gained valuable business and personal contacts throughout the Santa Barbara health care community.

PROFESSIONAL EXPERIENCE

Management & Supervision
* Supervised entire hospital evening nursing staff and became main source for troubleshooting among nursing professionals at St. Francis Hospital.
  - Responsible for overall nursing staff performance and total care of 100 bed facility.
  - Assured that family members were very well informed and involved.
* Supervised home health aides and private duty nurses for hospice home care. Successfully filled in as Director of Nurses in Directors absence.
* Charge nurse on a 40 bed surgical floor for six months.
  - Relief charge nurse of 32 bed floor in a 400 bed hospital for two years.
* Received extensive health care management training.

Hospice Home Care
* Expert in pain control and symptom management for five years.
  - Assessed patient's pain with ability to quickly determine best analgesic and method of delivery.
  - Thoroughly skilled in family dynamics to effectively counsel patients and offer emotional/spiritual support to terminally ill adults and their families.
  - Coordinate overall home care program with other community resources and services throughout Santa Barbara County.

Acute Emergency Assessment & Intervention
* Superior performance in intensive care unit for eight years: general..medical..surgical..coronary care..post trauma..neurological
  - Eight year member of the Code Blue Team, responding to cardiac arrest situations throughout the hospital.
  - Served as the only evening shift IV Therapist for three months at a 400 bed facility.
  - Assisted in the Emergency Room as needed.

PROFESSIONAL EXPERIENCE (Continued)

Foreign/Domestic Community Relations
* Volunteered as a Red Cross Nurse for five years.
* Educated parents as a PEP volunteer. (Post-Partum Education for Parents)
  - Served on the steering committee.
  - Developed a Baby Basics Class for expectant parents.
* Provided health care assistance in a remote clinic in Mexico as a World Health Volunteer.
  - Studied at the Jaime Balmes University in Saltillo, Mexico. Resided with a Mexican family.
* Volunteered through the American Heart Association. (Project Re-Entry)
  - Visited Stroke patients in their homes.
  - Coordinated outpatient therapy, arranged for supportive equipment and offered emotional support.

EDUCATION

AA Degree, Nursing, Sacramento City College, 1972
President, Chapter of the Student Nurses Association

EMPLOYMENT HISTORY

Hospice Nurse/Acting Director, Hospice of Santa Barbara Inc	1984-90
Relief Supervisor/Staff Nurse, St. Francis Hospital	1976-84
Evening Clinic Nurse, Outpatient Clinic, Sacramento, CA	1/76-7/76
IV Therapist/Charge & Staff Nurse, Mercy General Hospital	1972-75

Chapter VIII

ADDITIONAL RESUME SAMPLES
About the Additional Resume Samples

The following pages in this chapter consist of additional resume samples for women in many careers, each resume focusing on particular individual goals. You will see a variety of formats to choose from in functional and chronological styles. This chapter is divided into two sections.

- First is a variety of functional resume format samples.
- Second is a wide range of chronological resume format samples.

Look at each resume carefully. Again, think about how your own background applies to the job or internship you'd like to obtain.

REMEMBER, it's important that you've already read all the text in Chapters I, II & III before reviewing the resume samples in this chapter. This will give you the overall perspective you'll need to write an effective resume.

MEGAN AMANDA O'MALLEY
369 Pacific Coast Highway
Malibu, CA 90265
(213) 971-4443

OBJECTIVE

A challenging career in Portfolio Management.

PROFESSIONAL PROFILE

* Valuable business contacts in the bond market worldwide.
* Extensive knowledge of financial instruments.
* Thrive on new opportunities for accomplishment and success.
* Sharp analytic, problem solving and presentation skills.
* Team player with proven leadership qualities.
* Work well under highly pressured situations.
* Special talent for understanding client needs.

PROFESSIONAL EXPERIENCE

LOS ANGELES FIXED INCOME MANAGEMENT, Beverly Hills, CA   1980-90
Principal & Portfolio Manager/Trader

Portfolio Management
* Manage $5 billion of total-rate-of-return fixed income portfolios.
  - long duration...short duration...taxable...tax-exempt...sterling...individuals...nuclear decommissioning...immunization funds.
* Implement a highly disciplined investment process, flexible under all market conditions.
* In charge of active trading room and corresponding settlement operations.

Trading
* Maintain a sharply defined, critical mode of evaluating and analyzing fixed income investment instruments and strategies.
* Analyze and trade various fixed income securities:
  governments...municipals...foreigns...corporates...mortgages.
* Successfully evaluate yield curves, currencies, option adjusted spreads, duration and convexity.

Research Analysis & Evaluation
* Established an efficient credit research system.
* Organize client goals, objectives and restrictions.
* Monitor client characteristics.

EDUCATION

BA Degree, Business Economics, 1982
University of California, Los Angeles

References available upon request

-40-

NELCY KNUTSON, R.N.

6245 Olympic Blvd
Los Angeles, CA 90046
(213) 344-9999

Objective: Director of Nursing

PROFESSIONAL PROFILE

* Special talent in dealing with sensitive populations in a professional and concerned manner.
* Team leader with strength in adapting well to any situation with ability to quickly deliver the best nursing care possible.
* Highly organized, dedicated with a positive attitude.
* Outstanding written, oral and interpersonal communication skills.
* Bilingual skills; fluent in Spanish and Portuguese.
* Good working knowledge of Title 22, OSHA, JCAH, Health and Workmen's Compensation Insurance, MediCal/MediCare benefits.
* Member, California Nurses & American Nurses Associations.
* Received a Certificate in Medical-Legal Consulting.

PROFESSIONAL EXPERIENCE

Director of Nursing
* Directed and administered entire hospital nursing staffs and became main source for troubleshooting among nursing professionals at four hospitals.
  - Established cost-effective policy and procedures for three hospitals; improved patient care and resulted in a smoother flow of productivity.
  - Managed nursing and other administrative staff performance and total patient care for 40-175 bed facilities.
  - Assured that family members were very well informed and involved.
  - Coordinated financial budgets, cost analysis and purchasing.
* Developed and monitored patient care for performance of all medical treatment and services provided through a high Quality Assurance Program.
* Assessed and processed all MediCare and MediCal benefits.
* Provided extensive health care management training to nursing staff members of all levels.

Acute Emergency Assessment & Intervention
* Superior performance in critical care unit; general..medical..surgical..coronary care..post trauma..neurological..gerontological..open heart surgeries.
* Expert in management of pain control and hyperalimietation (TPN).
* Assessed patient's physiological, emotional and social needs.
  - Ability to quickly determine and perform the best care possible.
* Thoroughly skilled in family dynamics to effectively counsel patients and offer emotional/spiritual support to the terminally ill and their families.

Occupational Health Nurse
* Established and maintained health care programs for two manufacturing corporations each employing over 1500 employees for a one-nurse office.
  - Provided and performed emergency first aid, pre-employment physical examinations and Worker's Compensation cases on a daily basis.
  - Prepared and maintained all medical records and OSHA reports.

PROFESSIONAL EXPERIENCE

Occupational Health Nurse (Continued)
* Conducted in-house CPR and first aid classes for all employees.
* Developed safety programs and participated in Safety Committee meetings.
* Provided continued medical treatment, working closely with clinics and hospitals throughout the community.
* Performed services for the Rehabilitation Program and routine follow-up.
* Interacted with all levels of company management personnel in a highly professional and diplomatic manner.
* Purchased and maintained inventory and quality control of all clinical equipment and supplies.

EDUCATION

* **BS Degree, Psychology/Registered Nurse**
  University of Minas Gerais, Brazil
* **Adult Psychiatry in Nursing**
  University of California, San Francisco
* **Critical Care Nursing Certificate**
  West Valley College, Saratoga, CA
  Leadership, Supervision & Management
* **MBO Certificate, Business Administration**
  University of California, San Diego
* **Intensive Care/Rehabilitation**
  Santa Clara Valley Medical Center, SC, CA

EMPLOYMENT HISTORY

Director of Nursing, Mission Terrace Conv. Hosp., SB, CA		1989-90
Director of Nursing, Care West Santa Monica Conv. Hosp., SM, CA		1982-89
Occupational Health Nurse, Hiebert MFG Inc., Carson, CA		1981-82
Intensive Care Nurse, VA Hospital, Los Angeles, CA & Phoenix, AZ		1978-79
Director of Nursing, Carroll's SNF Lexington, San Diego, CA		1977-78
Primary Care Health Prac. Nurse, Sharp M. Rehab. Hosp., SD, CA		1976-77
Supervisor/Staff Nurse, Kaiser F. Hospital, Santa Clara, CA		1964-76

CHERYL A. JOHNSON
59 Martinella Drive
Montecito, CA 93108
(805) 966-0845

Objective: Trust Administrator

EDUCATION

Certified Financial Planner, 1990
College of Financial Planning, Denver, CO

Paralegal, Certified: 1982
The Institute of Paralegal Training
Philadelphia, PA

BA, Psychology/Business Administration
University of Arizona, Tucson, AZ, 1980
Summa Cum Laude

PROFESSIONAL EXPERIENCE

Trust Administration & Marketing
* Managed 180 accounts with total market value of $150M; revenues of $1.4M.
  Living...Testamentary...Conservatorship...Unitrusts...Agency...Custody.
* Launched intensive Cohen-Brown marketing techniques including financial
  profiling of existing client base, branch contact and organizing seminars.
* Organized highly successful in-house marketing campaigns that created
  excitement, promoted sales and generated new business for the bank.
* Conducted a week-long training seminar on new Trust Aid procedures for
  our updated in-house computer system.
* Prepared discretionary requests and monitored investments, distributions,
  terminations and sale of personal property.
* Portfolio manager for accounts fully vested in Common Trust Funds.
* Gained valuable business contacts through interbank communication and
  corresponding with attorneys, brokers, accountants in the trust industry.

Probate Paralegal
* Responsible for file management and factual investigation.
* Discovered, collected and distributed assets.
* Prepared and processed pleadings, federal/state estate, gift and inheritance
  tax and income tax returns, probate accountings and narrative descriptions
  pertaining to extraordinary services.
* Interfaced with secretarial, word processing, accounting and other support
  departments on a daily basis.

EMPLOYMENT HISTORY

Trust Administrator, Wells Fargo Bank, Santa Barbara/LA, CA	1987-present
Trust Administrator, Union Bank, Los Angeles, CA	1985-87
Probate Paralegal, Sheppard, Mullin, Richter, Hampton, LA, CA	1983-85
Probate Paralegal, Rooks, Pitts, Fullagar & Poust, Chicago, IL	1982-83

SUSIE M. MCDOWELL

i039 Beacon Hill
Boston, MA   02115
(619) 284-5551

OBJECTIVE

A <u>Trade Show Management</u> position for a National Magazine

EDUCATION

BA Degree, Graphics Art, 1988
<u>Boston University</u>, Boston, MA
Microcomputer Paste-up, Layout, & Design;
The Art of Interviewing; Travel Writing.

<u>Amherst College</u>, Amherst, MA, 1984
Journalism: Advanced Magazine/Specialty
Copywriting-Editing; Photography.

PROFESSIONAL EXPERIENCE

Writing, Editing & Production
* In charge of editing and coordinating the publication of corporate newsletter with a circulation of 4,000.
  - Developed story board and delegated selected articles to staff experts.
  - Selected artwork, took photos and produced layout for newsletter.
  - Coordinated projects with graphic designers, typesetters and printers meeting strict deadline schedules and budget requirements.
* Wrote, edited and produced promotional materials:
  letters...ads...news releases...brochures...directories...manuals...mailers.
* Three year member of the Boston Ad Club.

Trade Shows, Special Events & Meetings
* Coordinated and supervised national and regional trade shows for a multi-million dollar computer software company.
  - Developed and distributed materials that created interest, excitement and promoted sales.
  - Coordinated the entire set up: selected booth space, arranged staffing, chose graphic designs, lighting and furnishings.
* Organized special events and national training meetings.

Direct Mail Promotions & Lead Control
* Researched, compiled and selected appropriate direct mail lists.
* Supervised in-house and outside mailings of 500-40,000 pieces.
* Monitored and tracked responses to maintain the most cost effective promotional materials and lists.
* Supervised lead control: data entry of leads, generation of sales reports, development and distribution of literature packages to prospective clients.

EMPLOYMENT HISTORY

International Travel, Studies & Research	1989-90
Graphics/Editorial Manager, <u>Bostonian Magazine</u>, Boston, MA	1984-88
Corporate Communications Supervisor, <u>COMTECK</u>, Amherst, MA	1979-84

SUSAN ANNE WHEELER
Doctor of Oriental Medicine
Licensed Acupuncturist
1257 Grove Lane
Summerland, CA   93108
(805) 966-2456

EDUCATION

SAMRA Univ. of Oriental Medicine, LA, CA
Doctor of Oriental Medicine, 1986
Bachelor of Science Degree, 1983

Los Angeles City College, 1981-83
Biological Science

Graduate Studies,   Beijing, China, 1986
Qi Gong, Acupuncture

PROFESSIONAL EXPERIENCE

Chemical Dependency Program Development
* Instrumental in the development of the model for Turnaround, a group detox program sponsored by the LA County Sheriff and Police Depts.
* Developed and coordinated the first acupuncture group detox program in Los Angeles area for SAMRA University.
* Generated Outreach Program community support through newspaper, radio, and television resources.
* Organized and conducted educational presentations to social service agencies in residential rehab programs; located and invited guest speakers.
* Interviewed clients, outlined and set up personalized recovery programs.
* In charge of intakes, referrals, correspondence, purchasing, fees and case records.

Private & Group Detox-Acupuncture
* Administered in-house acupuncture and herbal treatment for the Skid Row population of 60-150 clients per day.
* Monitored clients with breathilizer and urine testing.
* Provided continued recovery treatment and referral service, working with law enforcement, social services and counselors throughout the community.
* Treated individuals and provided home detox care to private patients.
* Gained life experience from participating in family members' drug addiction and recovery process.
* Received "Outstanding Accomplishment" from the Mayor of Los Angeles for participation in the Turnaround Program - January, 1988.

Foreign-Group Therapy/Counseling
* Provided crisis intervention, brief and long term counseling to:
 - individual adults   -adolescents   -couples   -groups
* Dealt with clients of racial and economic diversity.
* Conducted group therapy series utilizing Peer Counseling or Bioenergetic techniques.
* Founding member of a 300 person skill training-work cooperative in London.

SPECIAL TRAINING

* California Acupuncture License #CA 1589 since 1983
* National Acupuncture Detox Assoc, Certified 1986
* Hypnotherapy Certification Board of California, 1983
* 7th & 8th Annual Institute on Drug & Alcohol Problems,
  UCLA Extension, 1986-87
* First Int'l Qi Gong Conference, Shanghai, China, 1986
* Acupuncture Detox Training Program, Lincoln Hospital of
  Bronx, New York, in Los Angeles, CA, 1982 & 1986
* Natural Medicine & Healing, private instruction, London,
  England, 1972-79
* Therapy & Counseling Training, London School of Bodymind
  Therapy, London, England, 1972-76
* Therapy Group Functions & Biofeedback Training,
  Quaesitor Institute, London, England, 1973
* Martial Arts Training, Kung Fu, Chu-Shin & Qi Gong,
  Beijing, China and Los Angeles, CA.
* Creative Writing/English Literature, Beloit College, 1970-72

EMPLOYMENT HISTORY

Licensed Acupuncturist, Health Spectrum, Santa Barbara, CA　　1989-present
Volunteer Acupuncturist, Turnaround (Detox Facility), LA, CA　　1986-88
Clinic Director/Acupuncturist, Wheeler Holistic Clinic, LA, CA　　1985-88
Clinic Coordinator, SAMRA University of Oriental Medicine, LA, CA　　1984-86

STEPHANIE JANE WILBER
Marriage, Family & Child Counselor
20450 Laguna Niguel Way
Santa Barbara, CA   93103
(805) 963-2393

PROFESSIONAL EXPERIENCE

Marriage, Family & Child Counseling
* Provide crisis intervention, brief and long term counseling to:
    -individual adults -adolescents -couples -families -groups
* Assess, diagnose and treat clients in major life transitions.
* Conduct group therapy series focused on peer counseling training, communication skills and self esteem.
* Educate, assess and counsel women who must decide between abortion, adoption or keeping the child.
* Faciliate all phases of open independent adoptions.
* Supply community referral resources.
* Coordinate intakes, referrals, correspondence, case records.

Chemical Dependency Counseling & Assessment
* Develop and implement primary education on predictable course of recovery for chemical dependency patients focusing on the following:
    Overview of addiction, indicators of potential relapse, self esteem, addiction as a family disease, denial, co-dependency and congruent communication.
* Counsel couples, individuals, families, family groups and adult children of alcoholics during their participation in a 12-Step Program.
* Educate and counsel battered women, demonstrating the relationship between substance abuse and family violence.

EDUCATION

MA Degree - Counseling Psychology - 1984
Pacifica Graduate Institute, Santa Barbara, CA

SPECIAL TRAINING

* California MFCC License #MFC24707 since 1988.
* Assessment and Treatment of Alcoholism.
* Assessment and Treatment of Adult Children of Alcoholics.
* Diagnosis and treatment of child abuse.
* Attended 7-day workshops; Jay Haley, Virginia Satir, Carl Whitaker, Salvador Minuchin and Claudia Black.
* Certified Massage Technician, Santa Barbara School of Massage, 1982.
* Gained knowledge through personal psychotherapy including:
    Couples Counseling and Gestalt Group Therapy.

EMPLOYMENT HISTORY

Adoption Counselor, Santa Barbara Adoption Center	5/89-present
Outpatient Chemical Dependency Therapist	
CPC Vista Del Mar Hospital, Ventura, CA	1/89-2/90
Substance Abuse Consultant, Shelter Services for Women, SB, CA	1/89-6/89
Relaxation Trainer, Cottage Care Center, Santa Barbara, CA	1988-89
Staff Counselor, Community Counseling Center, Santa Barbara, CA	1983-88

INEZ M. AYRES
7892 Forest Lane
Santa Barbara, CA 93105
(805) 966-9022

OBJECTIVE

A <u>Student Personnel Advisor</u> position in higher education

EDUCATION

* <u>MA, Student Personnel Service & Counseling</u>, 1975-79
  Trenton State College, New Jersey
* <u>MS, Administration</u>, 1972-74
  Fordham University, New York
* <u>BS, Elementary Education</u>, 1962-66
  St. Bonaventure University, New York
* <u>Certification</u>, St. Luke's Hospital School
  of Radiologic Technology, MA
* <u>Macintosh MacWrite, Microsoft Word</u>
  University of California, Santa Barbara 1990
* <u>Spanish in the Workplace, Word Perfect</u>
  Santa Barbara City College, 1990

PROFESSIONAL EXPERIENCE

Facilitator/Administrator
* Developed marketing strategies for the first Three-In-One Concepts programs throughout the Northeastern United States.
  - Became the main sponsor and source of information for...
  - training...seminars...workshops...private consultations...referrals.
* Conducted individual stress management consultation with clients.
* Presented Three-In-One Concepts professional development programs and special interest workshops to groups of 2-25 people.
  - Designed creative educational graphic materials.
  - Coordinated the entire set up: selected conference site, negotiated contractor fees, liaison between attendees and Three-In-One Concepts.
* Maintained public relations, appointment scheduling, bookkeeping, purchasing, inventory control and office management.

Chairperson - Higher Education
* Chairperson for the Radiography Education Dept. of a community college.
  - Interviewed and recommended individuals for faculty and clerical staff.
  - Developed and assigned schedules for faculty and student personnel.
  - Submitted budgetary requirements meeting strict deadline schedules.
  - Conducted monthly departmental staff meetings and periodic student orientation meetings.
  - Delegated committee tasks to faculty staff members and students.
* Coordinated education assignments with up to seven hospital affiliations throughout the state.
* Served as troubleshooter liaison between hospitals and the college.
* Contributed to the negotiation of guidelines for hospital/student contracts.
* Planned/organized review classes for the National Registry Examination.
  - Responsible for a significant college success rate increase.
* Served on various curriculum and student welfare committees.

PROFESSIONAL EXPERIENCE (Continued)

Teaching Faculty - Higher Education
* Taught radiography education courses in classroom, laboratory and hospital environments for groups of 4-35 community college students.
  - Human anatomy & pathology...radiographic positioning...medical ethics.
  - Designed specific courses including visual support materials.
  - Evaluated and graded students through observation and written testing.
* Advised and referred students concerning education, curriculum transfer, career options and personal issues.
* Assisted students with course registration procedures.
* Participated in monthly departmental, divisional and college wide meetings.

PUBLICATIONS

"The Ultimate Belief System," Int'l Association of Specialized Kinesiologists, Apr-89; "One Brain," HOLISTIC LIVING, Nov/Dec-86, Volume III, No. 6

SPECIAL TRAINING/CREDENTIALS

* Ericksonian Hypnosis Training, Eastern NLP Institute, 1988
* Three In One Concepts Facilitator, Burbank, CA, 1984-85
* Holistic Health Education, 1983
  Kripalu Center for Holistic Health, MA
* Licensed Radiologic Technologist LRT (R), 1965
  New York State Department of Health
* Licensed Radiologic Technologist LRT (R), 1973
  New Jersey Dept of Environment Protection
* Registered Radiologic Technologist ARRT (R)
  American Registry of Radiologic Technologists

EMPLOYMENT HISTORY

Facilitator/Administrator, CONCEPT TO REALITY, SB, CA		1984-present
Chairperson/Associate Professor, Middlesex County College, NJ		1973-84
Instructor, Hostos Community College, NY		1970-73

NANCY LYNN ROSTRON
5500 Deanna Street
Santa Barbara, CA   93103
(805) 966-4567

Objective: A Purchasing/Buyer position

PROFESSIONAL PROFILE

* Became main source of information because of proven ability to run a smooth efficient operation.
* Skill in maintaining optimum stock levels within strict budget.
* Efficiently work on several transactions simultaneously.
* Highly organized, dedicated with a positive attitude.
* Outstanding ability to communicate with vendors.
* Supervise employees with professionalism, diplomacy and tact.

PROFESSIONAL EXPERIENCE

Inventory & Purchasing
* Purchased all mechanical, electrical and fabricated supplies, equipment and chemical materials for entire Physics Department on a daily basis.
  - Successfully selected and qualified vendors; considered price, quality and shipping terms within the university policy and procedure restrictions.
  - Monitored invoices for accuracy of account coding.
  - Tracked expenditures for comparison with budgeted figures.
  - Managed shipping/receiving and returns; maintained storeroom and equipment inventory control for one of the largest departments on campus.
  - Interfaced daily with accounting, central purchasing, equipment management, central stores and central shipping/receiving departments.
  - Developed valuable personal contacts in the electronics industry working closely with fabricators, sheet metal shops, machine shops and electronic supply and component companies worldwide.

Organization & Management
* Hired, trained, supervised and streamlined storeroom department.
* Key member in converting manual procedures to an efficient computerized purchasing/inventory control system. Reorganized purchasing operations.
  - Identified and corrected the operational problems undermining efficiency.
  - Greatly increased the number of orders shipped daily.
  - Minimized the backlog of open orders.
  - Developed and implemented a user code system to track equipment and reduce errors in inventory recordkeeping; achieved high accuracy rate.
  - Set up and organized laboratories for newly hired professional staff.

EDUCATION

BA Degree, Speech and Hearing
University of California, Santa Barbara
Graduated: 1979   GPA: 3.3

EMPLOYMENT HISTORY

Purchasing Manager, UC Santa Barbara (Physics Dept), CA   1979-1990
Accounting Clerk, UC Santa Barbara (Physics Dept), CA   1976-1979

KRISTEN B. HARDY

3204 Kova Street
Santa Barbara, CA   93103
(805) 569-2201

Objective: A Management position in the Hospitality Field.

EDUCATION

AA Degree, Accounting, 1979
Santa Barbara City College

PROFESSIONAL EXPERIENCE

Hotel Management
* Started at the ground floor for the opening of a 5-star, 365 room, 24-acre oceanside hotel and resort.
* Served as source of information concerning needs of the Activities Dept.
  - Coordinated all promotional events and hotel activities.
  - Established Aqua/Jazzercise activities offered to public & hotel guests.
  - Organized group conventions in-house and on-location for 10-500 people.
  - Initiated cost effective poolside barbecues for hotel members.
* Participated in management meetings and conducted motivational staff meetings on a weekly basis.
* Hired, trained, supervised 20 employees, maintaining a positive attitude under highly stressful situations.

Restaurant Management
* In charge of all operations for a busy jazz club restaurant.
* Established better restaurant policies and procedures resulting in more efficient productivity to deal with employees and clientele on a daily basis.
* Prepared daily bookkeeping and accounting procedures.
* Hired, trained and supervised as many as 60 employees.

Food & Beverage/Catering
* Supervised and delegated staff of 150 employees for banquets serving 20-1000 guests. Involved set up and serving guests for the following: conventions...luncheons...theme parties...weddings...special events.
* Developed successful marketing strategies for radio advertising campaigns.
* Established dynamic theme parties, prepared and displayed decorations.
* Performed tableside food preparation.
* Liaison between management and clients, expediting challenges customers presented in a quick and creative manner.
* Gained thorough knowledge and skills through lifetime experience from a family catering service.

EMPLOYMENT HISTORY

Floor Manager, City Broiler, Santa Barbara, CA		1988-89
Act. Director/Bqt. Capt., Fess Parker's Red Lion Resort, SB, CA		1987-88
PR Director/Assist. Manager, The Famous Restaurant, Santa Barbara, CA & Colorado Springs, CO		1982-86

SUSAN E. PERLMAN

PO Box 5600
Albuquerque, NM 87109
(505) 821-2082

Objective: Research Historian

EDUCATION

MA Degree, History, 1989
New Mexico State University, Las Cruces, NM
Master's Thesis: "Livestock Policy of the Zuni
Indian Tribe: 1900-1942

Paralegal Certificate, 1983
Denver Paralegal Institute, Denver, CO

BS Degree, Environmental Interpretation, 1979
Colorado State University, Fort Collins, CO
Emphasis: Forestry

PAPERS PRESENTED

* "New Deal at Zuni: The Range Management Program,"
  Historical Society of New Mexico, Annual Conference, April, 1990
* "Zuni Indian Livestock Policy During the Early Twentieth Century,"
  Historical Society of New Mexico, Annual Conference, 1989.
* "Apache Scouts and the United States Army,"
  Phi Alpha Theta Regional Conference, 1988.

PROFESSIONAL EXPERIENCE

Research: Historical & Technical
* Prepared reports on natural resource utilization on Indian lands in New Mexico and Arizona.
  - Researched government documents, regulations, serial sets, archives, secondary sources.
  - Compiled, abstracted, and analyzed raw data.
  - Performed title searches in county and federal records.
* Coordinated court exhibits and data tables in preparation for submission of land claims report.
* Conducted historical research projects as a graduate research assistant.
* Performed legal research and administration of law library.
* Conducted technical research in the following fields:
  forestry...agriculture...animal husbandry...and hydrology.

Writing: Historical & Technical
* Wrote reports on Native American land and water utilization and rights for litigation use.
* Assembled annotated bibliographies for economic and resource study.
* Drafted pleadings for real estate, litigation, and estate administration.
* Composed and maintained correspondence with clients.

PROFESSIONAL EXPERIENCE (Continued)

Communication Experience
* Conducted extensive oral interviews; interviewees included Native American prison inmates, Native American livestock producers, alumnae for university centennial, legal and social services clients.
* Served as liaison between Native American self-help group and prison administration.
* Initiated development of cooperative programs with government agencies and community organizations.
* Worked closely with local, state, federal agencies and community groups.
* Established US Forest Service Visitor Center; responsible for development of exhibits.

Technical Experience
* Operate computers for database, writing, research, file management, and abstracting.
* Skilled interpreter of photographs and topographic maps.
* Maintained timber inventory and timber sale layout.
* Supervised timber field crews.

EMPLOYMENT HISTORY

Historian, Historical Research Associates, Missoula, Montana — 1989-90
Sponsor, Native American Council,
Southern New Mexico Correctional Facility, Las Cruces, NM — 1988-89
Research Assist, Institute of North American West, Albuquerque, NM — 1988
History Research/Teaching Assistant, New Mexico State University — 1987-89
Medicaid Elig Tech, Larimer Cty-Social Serv, Ft Collins, CO — 1984-86
Legal Sec/Paralegal, Remington Plaza Law Offices, Ft Collins, CO — 1984
Paralegal Intern, Environmental Defense fund, Boulder, CO — 1983
Forestry Tech, US Forest Service, Ft Collins, CO — 1979-81

REFERENCES AVAILABLE UPON REQUEST

SARA B. TAYLOR

1820 L Street
Lincoln, NE 68849
(402) 474-1110

Objective: An Interior Designer position.

DESIGN EXPERIENCE

Residential Interior Design Projects
* Successfully developed conceptual designs for several million dollar homes.
* Designed the interior of a 5000 square foot, Mediterranean style home.
  - Involved lighting, cabinet & kitchen design, ceiling and arch design.
* Designed interiors and finished surfaces for the exteriors of a 100-acre estate with a main house, guest house and stables.
* Developed the design concept through completion for a Beverly Hills home.
* Designed the interior of an estate on a 100 acre ranch outside, Omaha, NE.
* Successfully completed additional projects over the past eight years.

Communication Skills
* Developed presentation skills in drafting, rendering and material boards.
* Liaison between contractors, architects and clients, solving potential problems and meeting realistic demands at a fair price.
* Consulted with clients to interpret their needs and priorities for budget, color scheme, finished materials and space planning.

Project Management
* Oversaw, maintained and assisted the owner in remodeling an estate on the Santa Fe Ranch.
* Manage and operate a successful design consulting firm.
* Locate qualified vendors and negotiate contracts with subcontractors.
* Hire, schedule and supervise subcontractors. Developed and enforce effective company policy, procedures and project safety regulations.
* Purchase, expedite materials/equipment; maintain efficient quality control.
* Assist with light bookkeeping, working closely with the accountant.
* Maintained daily contact and on-site supervision.

EDUCATION

Environmental and Interior Design
Professional Certificate Program, Graduated: 1989
University of Nebraska Extension, Lincoln, NE

Environmental Conservation, 1976-78
University of California, Los Angeles

EMPLOYMENT HISTORY

Interior Designer, Kristin B. Taylor Designs, Lincoln, NE	1988-90
Ranch Manager, Rancho Santa Fe, Norfolk, NE	1983-88
Project Manager/Designer, Sierra Designs, Beverly Hills, CA	1980-81

BROOKE E. CHILCOTT, RN
6912 Cordova Court
Montecito, CA 93108
(805) 569-9992

Objective: A Utilization Review Nurse position.

PROFESSIONAL EXPERIENCE

Administration & Management
* Manage the Comprehensive Perinatal Services Program for Carpinteria and Franklin clinics.
* Supervise the assessment of designated patients for prenatal care:
  - physical...nutrition...psycho-social...and health education.
  - Monitor patient care and review documentation to determine accuracy and compliance with California State guidelines.
* Coordinate care for 350 on-going Hispanic and low income Prenatal and Postpartum patients.
* In charge of ordering and interpreting lab tests, triaging and appropriate follow-up within Santa Barbara County protocols.

Acute/Residential Nursing Care
* Performed daily plasmaphoresis for oncology patients at a 500-bed government/university hospital.
* Participated in the Oncology Department rounds to ensure appropriate care.
* Charge nurse for a 30-bed unit Chemical Dependency and Acute Medical/Surgical patients. Monitored care of short-stay surgical patients.
  - Liaison between patient, family and therapy staff and physicians.
  - Worked closely with PSRO, Medicare and SSI to provide documentation within their guidelines.
* Provided care to developmentally disabled patients in a 200-bed resident facility at the Devereaux School.
  - Developed individual health care program for residents.
  - Reviewed medical history for resident's admission.

Counselor/Educator
* Counseled and educated HIV testing individuals.
* Provided post pregnancy test counseling to women.
* Educated patients in Diabetes, PIH, AFP screening, PTL, RH sensitization.

EDUCATION

AA Degree, Nursing, Santa Barbara City College, 1975

LICENSE/PROFESSIONAL ORGANIZATIONS

California State Nursing License #A0000
Member, US-Mexico Border Health Association/WHO
Member, Healthy Mothers/Healthy Babies Coalition

EMPLOYMENT HISTORY

OB Clinic Manager, County of Santa Barbara	1983-90
Plasmaphoresis Nurse, Royal Hobart Hospital, Australia	Winter-Summer 1978
Staff Nurse, Devereaux School, Santa Barbara, CA	1975-76

PAULA L. KINNAIRD
Real Estate Associate
2954 Ignacio Lane
Montecito, CA 93108
(805) 569-0001

PROFESSIONAL PROFILE

* Highly organized, dedicated with a positive attitude.
* Special talent for assessing people's needs and priorities.
* Resourceful; skilled in analyzing and solving problems.
* Outstanding ability to communicate with all types of people.
* Work well under pressure situations maintaining a professional and concerned manner.
* Gained valuable business and personal contacts throughout the Santa Barbara community.

PROFESSIONAL EXPERIENCE

MERRILL LYNCH FINE HOMES, Montecito, California   May 1988-present
Real Estate Sales Associate

Real Estate Experience
* Exclusively sell <u>fine homes</u> throughout the Santa Barbara County.
  - Demonstrate strong visual insight and stage homes to obtain the best price for the seller and buyer.
  - Research computerized comparative analysis for appraisals.
* Attend City Council meetings to keep up with community projects...
  -condominiums -planned unit developments -new zoning ordinances

Client Relations
* Demonstrate poise and competence as a professional business representative in any social or business situation; work closely with elite clientele.
* Advise clients in a professional and concerned manner, securing their trust and confidence.
* Established a large personal customer base through thorough product knowledge, excellent sales ability and superior customer service; maintain continuous client follow up lists.

Sales & Promotions
* Evaluate territories to develop successful marketing strategies.
  - Distribute promotional newsletters to potential clients.
  - Arrange and conduct open houses on a weekly basis.
  - Identify inventory every week through the local newspaper.
  - Active bi-weekly caravan member to obtain the Hot Sheet for new listings.
  - Attend weekly sales meetings and seminars to keep up with the current marketplace and latest, innovative sales techniques.

EDUCATION

California Real Estate Salesman's License, 1988
Criminal Law, <u>Santa Barbara City College</u>, Honor Student

SANDI R. ORION
PO Box 2345
Santa Barbara, CA 93100
(805) 888-6789

OBJECTIVE

A <u>Post-Production</u> position in the <u>Television/Film Industry</u>.

PROFESSIONAL PROFILE

* Experienced in film production/post-production management.
* Highly organized, dedicated with a positive attitude.
* Strength in assessing people's needs and priorities.
* Outstanding ability to communicate with all types of people.
* Team player with proven leadership qualities and ability to supervise employees with professionalism, diplomacy and tact.
* Ability to handle multiple assignments in highly pressured situations and consistently meet tight deadline schedules.
* Traveled extensively throughout Japan, China, Europe, Canada, Mexico and the USA.

EDUCATION

BA Degree, Motion Picture - Spring 1988
<u>Brooks Institute of Photography</u>, Santa Barbara, CA

PRODUCTION EXPERIENCE

* Gained valuable knowledge and skills working closely with director and producer in all phases of film production.
  - Produced, directed, wrote and edited films; mixed sound tracks for several small narrative and documentary film productions.
* In charge of post-production; completed projects while consistently maintaining tight deadline schedules and strict budget requirements.

FILM & VIDEO PROJECTS

* <u>Producer</u> - "Freedom", a 15-minute documentary on the Homeless.
* <u>1st Assistant Camera</u> - "Circles", a rock style music video.
* <u>Head Editor</u> - "The Third World", a 15-minute documentary on Indonesia.
* <u>Script & Post-Production Supervisor</u>, "Non Compos Mentis", a 15-minute dramatic short. Psychological heart-beating thriller.
* <u>Assistant Camera/Editor</u> - "The Long Summer", Aired on NBC Summer 1989; a documentary, a sporty homebuilt airplane.
* <u>Producer</u> - "Rhythms", an animated 3-minute music video.

REFERENCES & PORTFOLIO

Available upon request.

BRITTINY A. SUMMERS

690 10th Street
Boulder, CO 80302
(303) 449-1123

Objective: A Price Analyst position.

PROFESSIONAL PROFILE

* Highly organized, dedicated with a positive attitude.
* Ability to handle multiple assignments in highly pressured situations and consistently meet tight deadline schedules.
* Thorough and committed to professionalism; thrive on opportunities to assume responsibility.
* Good written, oral and interpersonal communication skills.
* Completed extensive auditing workshops & self-study courses.

PROFESSIONAL EXPERIENCE

Proposal Audit/Incurred Cost Audit
* Successfully perform audits of small and intermediate contractors throughout Santa Barbara as an active member of the mobile team.
 - Evaluate proposals to determine reasonableness, accuracy and compliance with government regulations.

Labor Floor Check
* Review contractors labor charging and allocation system to determine the adequacy of contractor's labor policies, procedures and internal controls.
 - Recommend improvements to comply with government regulations.

Accounting System Review
* Analyze contractors accounting systems and internal controls to determine adequacy of accumulating and segregating costs for government contracts.

EDUCATION

BS Degree, Business, Accounting Emphasis
University of Colorado, Boulder, CO, 1987

AA Degree, Business Economics, 1984
Kinsborough Community College, Brooklyn, NY

EMPLOYMENT HISTORY

Auditor, Boulder Bank & Trust, Boulder, CO	1988-90
Home Management, Travel, Study	1982-88
Sales Representative, Joslyn College Division, Ft Collins, CO	1975-82

MARYL COOK

324 Central Park East
New York, NY   10038
(212) 799-4002

Objective: A Communications Management position

PROFESSIONAL EXPERIENCE

Public Relations/Communications
* Contact clients at location sites on a daily basis to counsel, advise and assess specific needs for advertising services of the daily newspaper.
  - Outstanding ability to solve problems under highly pressured situations in a professional and concerned manner.
* Member of staff Newsletter and Recreation Committees. Plan and coordinate internal social events, promotional projects and the entire newsletter.
* Marketing Committee Member at the Santa Barbara YMCA.
  - Compose press releases and public service announcements to publicize special events for this nationwide non-profit organization.
  - Successfully gain radio media and local business sponsorships.

Project Development
* Develop highly successful marketing strategies and corporate identities.
  - Design logos, brochures and copywrite for newspaper/radio advertising.
  - Establish excellent rapport with sales representatives throughout the advertising and publications industry locally and nationwide.
* Achieved the highest spec ad sales rating in the history of the art department of the daily newspaper publication. Increased monthly sales by 20%.

Director/Coordinator
* Coordinate, prioritize and implement multiple projects efficiently; consistently meet tight deadline schedules under daily pressure situations.
* Locate qualified vendors to purchase equipment and supplies under strict corporate budget requirements.
* Quality Assurance Board Member; monitor daily paper and magazine quality.
* With thorough knowledge on the Macintosh computer, became main source of information for The New York Times staff.
* Interview, train and supervise creative staff members.

EDUCATION

BA Degree, Graphic Communications, 1985
University of Florida, Gainesville, FL

EMPLOYMENT HISTORY

Art Director, The New York Times, New York, NY	1988-present
Commercial Artist, Orange Coast Magazine, Florida, CA	1987-88
Graphic Artist, Carlson Color Graphics, Ocala, FL	1986-87

JACQUELINE ANN FRANK

301 Victoria Court
Asheville, NC 28801
(704) 254-9992

Objective: A Flight Attendant position

PROFESSIONAL EXPERIENCE

Estate Nanny
* Provided total care for 2-3 children from infant to age 6 for several prominent families since 1971.
* Prepared and served meals to the children.
* Planned children activities and daily outings.
* Shopped, ran family errands and maintained light housekeeping.
* Supervised children while traveling on family vacations.

Montessori Teacher's Aide
* Assisted teacher with classrooms of 30 students ages 2-6.
* Set up daily classroom and outdoor activities i.e, drama workshops, sports, arts & crafts and singing; prepared lunches and snacks.
* Motivated children to maximize participation and enjoyment.
* Learned to deal in emergency situations quickly and efficiently.

Sales Representative
* Sold educational training programs to individuals for a business college.
* Conducted sales presentations, demonstrating poise and confidence while speaking to small groups of people.
* Oversaw efficient, courteous and friendly service, expediting challenges students presented in a quick and creative manner.
* Interviewed prospective students, issued aptitude test and gave a tour of the school; collected enrollment fee.
* Prepared and maintained appointment schedules and sales reports, meeting strict deadline schedules on a daily basis.

Receptionist/Cashier
* Demonstrated excellent public relations skills while providing customer service at a busy retail drug store chain.
* Maintained accuracy and speed while balancing daily cash transactions.
* Stocked shelves and maintained cleanliness at the end of the day.
* Answered 15 multi-phone lines for 3 doctors and nurse practitioners.
* Worked on multiple assignments under pressured situations maintaining a highly professional and concerned manner.
* Greeted patients and scheduled appointments on a daily basis.

EMPLOYMENT HISTORY

Estate Nanny, Ms. Carla Simmons, Asheville, NC	1989-90
Teacher's Aide, Montessori Center School, Asheville, CA	1987-88
Sales Representative, SB Business College, Santa Barbara, CA	1986-87
Receptionist, Sansum Medical Clinic, Santa Barbara, CA	1983-84
Cashier, Longs Drug Store, Santa Barbara, CA	1982-83

JOANNA HOUSTON
Marriage, Family & Child Counselor
3000 Southwest Park Road
Portland, OR 97219
(503) 293-0009

PROFESSIONAL PROFILE

* Over 10 years professional experience as a Psychotherapist.
* Special talent for dealing with sensitive populations in a professional and concerned manner.
* Concerned with the <u>total</u> growth and needs of the client.
* Team player/leader, dependable, flexible and efficient.

CLINICAL EXPERIENCE

JOANNA HOUSTON, MFCC, Portland, OR   1978-present

Marriage, Family & Child Counseling
* Provide crisis intervention, brief and long term counseling to:
  -individual children -adolescents -adults -couples -family -groups
* Conduct group therapy sessions focused on assertiveness training, communication skills, self esteem and life transitions.
* Deal with clients of diverse backgrounds specializing in sandtray, dreamwork, art, journal exploration and authentic movement.

Grief: Life, Death & Transition Therapy
* Effectively counsel clients and offer emotional and spiritual support by maximizing participation in sharing grief experiences.
  - Educate clients on the basic tools necessary to accept and deal with loss and change.
  - Provide options to motivate sense of well being, positive growth and self-development.

EDUCATION

* <u>MA Degree, Counseling Psychology</u> - 1978
  Western College, Portland, OR
* <u>BA Degree, Psychology</u> - 1966
  Queens College, Charlotte, NC

SPECIAL TRAINING

* <u>Oregon MFCC License #1000000</u> since 1980.
* In-depth seminar, **Life, Death & Transition**, <u>Elisabeth Kubler-Ross</u>.
* Attended 10-day, **Jungian Conferences**, <u>Life meaning & individuation</u>.
* Personal psychotherapy includes: Jungian Analysis, Gestalt Therapy, Couples Counseling, Sandtray Therapy, Authentic Movement Therapy, Intensive Journal Process. 1978-present
* Hospice Training for Volunteers. 1977

PROFESSIONAL AFFILIATIONS

* Member, Oregon Assoc. of Marriage & Family Therapists.
* Member, National Board for Certified Counselors.

ZORAH A. HURD
6390 Central Park East
New York, NY 10021
(212) 431-0002

Objective: Sales Management position for a Fine Arts Gallery

PROFESSIONAL PROFILE

* 25 years experience in all phases of fashion and editorial design and management in retail, advertising industries.
* Excellent written, oral, interpersonal communication skills.
* Problem solver/team player with proven leadership qualities.
* Invited to display artwork at many private and public shows nationwide. Won several awards.

EDUCATION

Editorial/Fashion Illustration, Parsons School of Design, NY

PROFESSIONAL EXPERIENCE

Design and Illustration
* Designed/illustrated original artwork on greeting cards and 3-dimensional ornamental designs for accredited Scandinavian department store and several design firms.
* Designed artwork for engravers of Steuben Glass Fine Arts Crystal.
* Traveled to major fashion shows throughout New York City to design and illustrate the fashion booklet for Associated Merchandising Corporation.
* Coordinated fashion/accessories for photographer in the fashion catalog.
* Displayed original acrylic paintings at art shows/galleries nationwide.

Management and Administration
* Managed and supervised employees at a busy antique shop in Corning, NY.
  - Hired, trained and supervised a staff of four employees.
  - Buyer of antique, vintage clothing and mid-century designs.
  - Maintained inventory/quality control, merchandising, shipping/receiving, accounts payable and receivable, payroll, banking and cash management.

Promotions & Customer Relations
* Designed interior and window displays that promoted sales.
* Developed successful advertising campaigns.
* Illustrated fashion and accessories of fine women's clothing store for advertising, promotions and sales.
* Expedited challenges customers presented in a quick and creative manner.
* Established a large personal customer base and created and maintained a "Preferred Customer List" that included customer follow up.

EMPLOYMENT HISTORY

Sales Manager/Buyer, The Sow's Ear, Corning, New York	1975-90
Greeting Card Designer, Bergdorf Goodman, New York City, NY	Freelance
Engraving Designer, Steuben Glass, New York City, NY	Freelance

RUTH ROUSSEAU
569 San Simeon Road
Ventura, CA 93003
(805) 656-3250

Objective: A Receptionist/Administrative Assistant position

PROFESSIONAL PROFILE

* 10-years experience as receptionist, general office with superior customer relation skills.
* Highly organized, dedicated with a positive attitude.
* Excellent written/oral & interpersonal communication skills.
* Ability to work on multiple assignments under pressure situations and consistently meet deadline schedules.

OFFICE SKILLS

IBM PC...DisplayWrite IV word processing...computerized billing...ten key adding machine...data entry...excellent phone skills...filing. Typing speed: 45 wpm

PROFESSIONAL EXPERIENCE

Communication Skills
* Key member in the installation of a customized ROLM phone system for IBM Corporation.
  - Worked closely with sales reps, management and technicians to establish Phone Mail system.
  - Responsible for all Phone Mail functions.
* Quick and efficient on the ROLM answering multiphone line system for two locations and 100 extensions.
  - Screen phone calls, expediting challenges customers presented in a highly professional manner.
* Responsible for answering customer and staff inquiries regarding to department rules, regulations and procedures.
* Scheduled appointments and travel arrangements for management staff.

Office & Organizational Skills
* Typed correspondence and memos on the word processor.
* Scheduled appointments for management staff.
* Maintained inventory control and purchased departmental supplies.
* Updated and maintained library manuals and policy/procedure manuals on a timely basis.
* Ordered IBM manuals for in-house staff members and customers.
* Processed orders and computerized billing.

EMPLOYMENT HISTORY

Secretary/Receptionist, IBM Corporation, Santa Barbara, CA	1984-1990
Sales Associate, Frazee Paint, Santa Barbara, CA	1983-84
Account Clerk, Cty of Santa Barbara, (Auditor-Controller)	1981-82
Research Assistant, Professor William Madsen, UCSB, CA	1980-81

KAREN J. PETERSON
222 Blanca Lane
Santa Fe, NM 85702
(505) 471-0489

Objective: A Bookkeeping position with a reputable firm.

EDUCATION

Business Administration, 1988-89
Santa Fe Community College, Santa Fe, NM

California Teaching Credential, 1983
California State University, Chico, CA

BS Degree, Education, 1969
Brigham Young University, Provo, UT

OFFICE SKILLS

Ten key by touch...accounts receivable...accounts payable...
general ledgers and journals...payroll...bank reconciliation...
balance sheets...trial balance...computer skills...Microsoft Word
and Word Perfect word processing...excellent phone, customer and
employee relation skills...typing: 55 wpm.

PROFESSIONAL EXPERIENCE

Management & Bookkeeping
* Assisted in establishing a structure for a growing company.
  - Set up and maintained bookkeeping procedures for accounts receivable, payable and general ledgers.
* In charge of managing three very service-oriented McDonald's Restaurants.
  - Prepared detailed labor cost and analysis, weekly statistical reports and analyzed annual profit and loss statements.
  - Conducted monthly motivational and educational staff meetings.
  - Performed weekly accounting procedures for accounts receivable, payable and inventory control.
  - Hired, trained and supervised 60 employees at each location.

Community Relations & Promotions
* Developed in-house theme campaigns that successfully promoted sales.
* Promoted fundraisers through local business sponsorships and donations.

EMPLOYMENT HISTORY

Home Management, Travel, Studies	1984-present
6-7 Grade Teacher, Richmond School District, Susanville, CA	1979-86
Manager, McDonald's Corporation, Seattle, WA	1977-79
K-2 Grade Teacher, Granite School District, Salt Lake City, UT	1969-77
Bookkeeper, California Liquid Gas Corp, Sacramento, CA	Summers 1965-75

KIMBERLY ANN RUSSELL, C.P.A.

23501 Brody Street
San Francisco, CA 94125
(415) 967-1145

EDUCATION

Golden Gate University, Summer 1990
TA 318 Federal Income Taxation for Individuals

BS Degree, Business Administration, 1986
Cal Poly State University, San Luis Obispo, CA
Concentration: Accounting

AS Degree, Business Economics, 1982
Northern Arizona University, Flagstaff, AZ

PROFESSIONAL ORGANIZATIONS

American Institute of Certified Public Accountants
California Society of Certified Public Accountants;
(organized Channel Counties Chapter CPE Programs)

PROFESSIONAL EXPERIENCE

1986-present

BARSTOW RALSTON & WILEY, San Francisco, CA
Staff Accountant
* Prepare various types of complex tax returns.
* Examine compilations, reviews and audits.
* Serve as client service representative for a number of the firm's clients.
* Developed increased technical knowledge in various areas of taxation and accounting.
* Increased my ability to supervise staff members.
* Learned the importance of efficiency and chargeability.

1985-86

ROBERT C. BARKLEY, C.P.A., San Luis Obispo, CA
Accounting Assistant
* Prepared accounts receivable and payable, monthly billing statements and payroll.
* Assisted accountants in the preparation of financial statements for various clients.
* Developed a clear image of the accounting process and moderate exposure to computer usage.

1983-84

APPLIED SCIENCE CORPORATION, San Luis Obispo, CA
Cost Accounting Assistant
* Assisted product line controller in preparation of labor variance reports and departmental forecasts.
* Generated reports for annual audit.

REFERENCES AVAILABLE UPON REQUEST

KARLA J. CAMPBELL
1256 Rocky Lane
Boulder, CO 85721
(303) 872-4444

OBJECTIVE

<u>Sales/Marketing Representative</u> for a pharmaceutical company

EDUCATION

BA Degree, Political Science, June 1990
<u>University of Colorado</u>, Boulder, CO

Semester at Sea Program, March-June 1982
<u>University of Pittsburgh</u>
Around the world studies (12 countries)

RELATED PROFESSIONAL EXPERIENCE

BOULDER COTTAGE HOSPITAL, Boulder, CO   1990-present
Pharmacy Technician
* In charge of work flow for 16 technicians in the pharmacy department of a busy 6-floor, 400+ bed hospital.
* Key member in converting manual procedures to a highly sophisticated computerized pharmacy system.
  - Developed effective training methods for staff members.
  - Organized/conducted training sessions for technicians and pharmacists.
* Prepared/distributed unit dose & intravenous drugs for all nursing units.
* Interpreted and clarified physicians' orders with attention to detail.
* Served as liaison between pharmacists, physicians and nurses to insure accuracy and safety of pharmaceutical procedures for patients.
* Worked on multiple projects simultaneously under highly pressured situations and consistently met strict deadline schedules.

FT COLLINS PLAZA DRUG, Ft Collins, CA   1982-89
Pharmacy Technician/Cashier/Sales
* Answered customer inquiries and developed a large personal customer base, demonstrating thorough product knowledge and excellent customer service.
* Accurately typed prescriptions into the computer. Thoroughly familiar with medical terminology.
* Prepared claims for Medi-Cal and Health Net insurance customers.
* Position required purchasing, inventory/quality control, cash management, filing and phone skills with ability to work well under pressure situations in a professional and concerned manner.

PREVIOUS EXPERIENCE

Administrative Assist., <u>Univ. of Pittsburgh</u>, Semester at Sea	Spring 1982
Sales Associate, <u>Paradise Drug</u>, Paradise, CA	1981-82
Home Management, Research, Study	1975-81

MOLLY RACHEL MCKINSEY

5720 Green Street
San Francisco, CA 94750
(415) 450-2378

Objective: To successfully market nonprofit organizations

EDUCATION

MBA, <u>University of Santa Clara</u>, Santa Clara, CA, December 1984
Emphasis: Marketing and Finance

BA, French Literature, <u>UC Berkeley</u>, Berkeley, CA, June 1980
Phi Beta Kappa

EXPERIENCE

AMERICAN LIBRARY, Geneva Switzerland   1987-90
Publicity Coordinator (volunteer position)
- Developed marketing program.
- Wrote magazine articles and radio announcements.
- Organized direct mail program.
- Designed and produced brochure for new members.
- Managed advertising campaign for annual booksale.
- Gave presentations to community groups.

WELLS FARGO BANK, San Francisco, CA   1985-87
Project Manager
- Managed implementation of the Wells Fargo/Crocker overdraft class action suit settlement, including 22 sub-projects and a $1,000,000 budget.
- Served as liaison between Consumer Marketing, Credit Card, Legal, Operations, Systems, and Public Relations departments.
- Coordinated development and production of customer communications.
- Awarded bonus and letter of commendation at completion of project.

Associate Product Manager
- Managed summer advertising campaign for checking accounts.
- Researched proposal for an upscale customer service program.
- Developed conversion plan for Crocker certificate of deposit accounts for the Wells Fargo/Crocker Bank merger.
- Edited and coordinated branch training materials.

Assistant Product Manager
- Analyzed interest rates and presented pricing recommendations to senior management on a weekly basis.
- Wrote monthly business reviews and marketing proposals.
- Researched and analyzed competitive products and institutions.
- Wrote telemarketing scripts and assisted with telemarketing training.
- Created and managed branch incentive campaign.

EXPERIENCE (Continued)

CLAIROL INC, Oakland, CA   1981-84
Sales Representative
- Responsible for selling Clairol haircare products directly to major drug store chains and mass merchandisers, e.g. Longs, KMart.
- Achieved 15 percent annual increase for San Francisco-Sunnyvale sales territory.
- Designed and installed haircolor department layouts and displays.
- Presented new products, major promotions and business reviews.
- Provided personalized customer service and follow-up.

EMPORIUM-CAPWELL, Fremont, CA   1980-81
Department Sales Manager
- Trained, supervised and motivated sales staff of 15 employees.
- Analyzed sales trends and established sales goals.
- Negotiated procurement of best-selling items with central buying office.
- Redesigned layout of sales floors to emphasize faster growing businesses.

SPECIAL SKILLS

- Fluent in French (Diploma, University of Geneva, July 1988)
- Proficient on IBM and Macintosh PC's (Lotus 1-2-3, Microsoft Word)

REFERENCES AVAILABLE UPON REQUEST

MARIE HECKENDORN

30566 Spruce Street
Santa Barbara, CA   90103
(805) 569-2290

OBJECTIVE

A position in leading to a career in Television News Broadcasting

EDUCATION

BA Degree, Law & Society, June 1990
University of California, Santa Barbara
Member, Pre Law Association
Dean's Honor List: Fall 1987   GPA: 3.20

Study Abroad Program, 1988-89
Syracuse University, Madrid, Spain
Speak fluent Spanish

Extracurricular Courses:
Photography...Acting...Drama...Modeling

RELATED EXPERIENCE

KCTV, (COX) CHANNEL 19, Santa Barbara, CA   1990-present
Studio Production/Camera Operation
* Received intensive hands-on training in all phases of studio production and camera operations including the teleprompter.

CENTRAL COAST MODEL & TALENT, San Luis Obispo, CA   1989-present
Model, Actress, Personal Development Student
* Received training in print, commercial and runway modeling techniques.
* Developed effective communication skills, telephone and selling techniques, social etiquette, fitness & nutrition and makeup application.
* Gained valuable acting techniques for television, commercial, soap, sitcom and film.

ABC TV STATION, New York City, NY   1989-90
Production Intern
* Received training in television production techniques during several airings of the Good Morning America show.

EMPLOYMENT HISTORY

Front Desk/Sales, Sundance Tanning Studio, Santa Barbara, CA 1989-present
Front Desk/Phone Sales, Nutri-System, Santa Barbara, CA   1989-90
Law Secretary, P. Heckendorn, Lawyer, San Marino, CA   Summers 1985/87

DIANA SUZANNE PARKER
56 West End Avenue
New York, NY 01002
(212) 324-0001

JOB OBJECTIVE

Features Reporter for a newspaper that values
tenacity, dependability, and creativity.

PROFESSIONAL EXPERIENCE

NEW YORK TIMES, New York, NY
Lifestyles Writer, 1986-present
General features include: current events, personality profiles, business and
tourism. Entertainment articles range from film, theater and book reviews to
celebrity interviews, previews and humor.

AMERICAN FILM, Hollywood, CA
Freelance Writer, Summer 1985
Wrote film and television articles. American Film is a national magazine of the
film and television arts, published by The American Film Institute. Several
articles were translated and re-published in Jaioliu, a film magazine from the
People's Republic of China.

DAILY NEWS RECORD, Harrisburg, VA
Features Writer 1982-84
Assigned to features and lifestyles. The Daily News Record is an AM daily
with a circulation of 31,000.

THE DAILY REFLECTOR, Greenville, NC
Associate Editor/Staff Writer, 1980-82
Assigned to general features, news and entertainment. The Daily Reflector
has a circulation of about 23,000.

GOOD TIMES
Contributor/Columnist, 1975-80
Contributed book and film reviews, social commentary and general features.
Wrote "Off the Cuff," a question and answer column covering any topic.
Good Times, is a Santa Cruz bi-weekly entertainment magazine with a cir-
culation of about 18,000.

SANTA BARBARA MAGAZINE
Contributor, 1973-75
Wrote features, personality profiles and the column, "Focus," a look at entre-
preneurs and new businesses. Santa Barbara Magazine is a four-color city
magazine with a circulation of 10,000.

Other features published in The Santa Barbara News-Press, The Santa Barbara News & Review and Connexions, a literary magazine.

EDUCATION

MA Degree, Journalism, University of California, Berkley, CA, 1980
BA Degree, English, University of California, Santa Barbara, CA, 1976

SUSAN A. COX
5112 Parkridge Lane
Thousand Oaks, CA   90266
(818) 342-9099

OBJECTIVE: A challenging career expanding my Human Relations skills, working with <u>Marine Mammals and other Exotics</u>.

PROFESSIONAL PROFILE:

* 10 years experience as back office medical technician/transcriptionist; proficient in medical terminology.
* Deal with the unexpected effectively with strong sense of responsibility and initiative.
* Highly organized, dedicated with a positive attitude.
* Excellent oral and written communication skills.
* Ability to cultivate relationships with people of various professional and personal backgrounds.
* Speak with poise and confidence in front of groups of people.
* Served as guest speaker on local TV station representing Exotic Animal Program and guest lecturer for community organizations.
* Participated in televised broadcasts and photography layouts for various media events.

EDUCATION:

* <u>BA Degree, Behavioral Psychology</u>, in-progress
  California State College, Northridge, CA
* <u>Designated Subject Credential</u>, 1988
  Cal Lutheran, Thousand Oaks, CA
* <u>AS Degree, Exotic Animal Training & Mgmt</u>, 1987
  Moorpark College, Moorpark, CA
* <u>Psychology/Business Administration</u>, 1986
  Ventura Community College, Ventura, CA
* <u>Cert. of Achievement, Exotic Animal Care & Handling</u>
  Moorpark College, Moorpark, CA, 1985

EXOTIC ANIMAL EXPERIENCE:

1985-present

EXOTIC ANIMAL TRAINING & MGMT PROGRAM, Moorpark College
Community Education Coordinator/Instructor
Provide diet planning and implementation, veterinary care and first aid for 150 species of birds, mammals and reptiles. Supervise and manage students in wildlife care and maintenance. Instruct and assist students with training and upkeep of behaviors on marine and terrestrial exotics and domestics. Update animal inventory including medical records and Int'l Species Inventory System. Prepare reports, permits and license requests. Guide public relation tours and correspond with the media, public and private organizations. Serve as instructor for Animal Training and Advanced Education and Entertainment in Animal Parks. Organize and execute educational animal presentations for public and private organizations. Programmer and MC for public educational services. Coordinate and implement animal assisted therapy programs for the mentally and physically handicapped. Represent staff at conferences, seminars, lectures and workshops. Serve as office assistant/liaison for director of EATM Program.

EXOTIC ANIMAL
EXPERIENCE: (Continued)

June 1988   SAN DIEGO ZOO'S WEGEFORTH BOWL
                     Trained with head trainer of seals and sea lions.

February 1988   DOLPHIN QUEST, The Big Is., Hawaii
                     Assisted with capture of wild dolphins in the Florida Panhandle.
                     Included transport, medical work-ups, initial care and training.

1985-86   MARINELAND OF THE PACIFIC, Rancho Palos Verdes, CA
                     Volunteer Assistant
                     Assisted with basic care and medical work-ups. Observed tech-
                     niques of trainers and veterinarians working with seals, sea lions,
                     walruses, dolphins, penguins and sea birds.

Summer 1985   SANTA BARBARA ZOOLOGICAL GARDENS, Santa Barbara, CA
                     Zookeeper
                     Provided infant care of exotics, diet preparation/distribution.
                     Responsible for animal lock up and closure of zoological facility.

1983-85   EXOTIC ANIMAL TRAINING & MGMT PROGRAM, Moorpark, CA
                     Zookeeper
                     Responsible for all aspects of exotic and domestic animal care
                     including diet preparation/distribution, record keeping, daily
                     sanitation, cage construction and repair. Served as apprentice
                     Zookeeper at the Santa Barbara and Los Angeles Zoos. Performed
                     behavioral research studies of mammals and birds. Provided infant
                     care of various exotic and domestic mammals and birds.

                     Animal Trainer
                     Raised and trained Bengal Tigers and Rhesus Macaques, Psitta-
                     cines and other species of carnivores, herbivores and primates.
                     Participated in educational animal presentations for public and
                     private organizations with above animals and birds.

AFFILIATIONS
CERTIFICATIONS: Member of:
                     American Association of Zoological Parks and Aquariums (AAZPA)
                     Int'l Marine Animal Trainers Association, (IMATA)
                     Int'l Zoo Educators, (IZE)
                     American Association of Zookeepers, (AAZK)
                     Greater Los Angeles Zoo Association, (GLAZA)
                     San Diego Zoological Society
                     National Marine Educators Association, (NMEA)
                     The Society for Marine Mammalogy
                     Delta Society & Special Olympics
                     Cardiopulmonary Resuscitation
                     Special Olympic Equestrian Therapy Training
                     Open Water Scuba Certified/Safety Diver - (NAUI)

Willing to Relocate

KATHERINE ANN WILEY

4590 Mountain Creek Road
Oceanside, CA 90266
(619) 630-4582

OBJECTIVE

A position in an OB/GYN clinic environment

PROFESSIONAL EXPERIENCE

FETAL MONITORING SERVICES, San Diego, CA   1990-present

Antepartum Consultant
* Perform 25-50 non-stress tests per month for the County of San Diego and provide testing for several private physicians.

GENERAL HOSPITAL, San Diego, CA   1977-present

Obstetrical & Out-Patient Nurse
* Provided total patient care and support and during the antepartum, labor and delivery process for eight years.
  - Counsel and educate patients in labor, post partum and newborn care.
  - Assessed and triaged incoming labor patients.
  - Assisted doctor with delivery and provide immediate newborn care.
  - Managed obstetrical emergency intervention.
* Provide total to post partum and long-term antepartum patients on the mother infant unit.
* Provided complete care for short-term surgery patients...
  Admitting...circulating...recovering...discharge planning.

Administration & Management
* Charge nurse for the labor and delivery unit; 120-160 births per month.
  - Supervised and scheduled a staff of 18 nurses.
  - Interviewed, hired and oriented new personnel.
* Oversaw the Antepartum testing unit.
  - Assisted in developing effective antepartum policies and procedures.
  - Performed NSTs, OCTs, BSTs and assisted with fetal versions and Amnio-centesis'.

EDUCATION

BS Degree, Nursing, 1974
Humboldt State University

LICENSE/CERTIFICATES/AFFILIATIONS

* California State Nursing License #678910
* Public Health Certificate, #1234
* Treasurer/Co-Founder, San Diego County
  Chapter of NAACOG; Awarded "Nurse of the
  Year for 1990.

PAMELA TAPIA
Illustrator...Line Art...Cartoons
3490 Sandy Lane
Santa Barbara, CA 93103
(805) 964-2663

**PROFESSIONAL
PROFILE:**

* Artist specializing in realistic & cartoon black & white line art.
* Highly organized, dedicated with a positive attitude.
* Work quickly and efficiently under highly pressured situations while consistently meeting tight deadline schedules.

**PUBLISHED
WORK:**

Tangerine Press - Illustrated the front cover and throughout the book titled "The College Student's Resume Guide." Written by Kim Marino.

Avery Press - Illustrated realistic cartoon drawings for the entire book titled "Computers & Small Fry." Written by Mario Pagononi.

Avery Press - Illustrated realistic line drawings for the chapter headings of the book titled "Shopper's Guide to Natural Food." Written by the Editors of the Far West Journal.

Avery Press - Illustrated technical & soft mood drawings for "Breast-feeding Today." Written by Candice Woessner, Judith Lauwers and Barbara Bernard.

Avery Press - Illustrated line drawing for the Canadian book "Having Babies." Written by Toula Hatherall.

Avery Press - Illustrated cartoon drawings throughout the book "Lamaze is For Chickens." Written by Mimi Green and Maxine Naab.

**CLIENTS/
PROJECTS:**

Ray's Liquor - Illustrated a drawing of the store front on a tee shirt for company promotions.

Santa Cruz Markets - Designed and illustrated three promotional tee shirts two store locations.

Ed's Bait & Tackle - Designed and illustrated tee shirts mass produced for in-house promotions and sales.

Visitor Press - Designed and illustrated two maps involving historical and tourist sites of Santa Barbara. Illustrated an in-house display that captured excitement and promoted sales.

Brown Pelican Restaurant - Designed and illustrated a promotional matchbook cover and the dinner menu for this fine dining restaurant.

HEIDI ELIZABETH SANDLER
210 Chelsey Road
Toluca Lake, CA   95102
(818) 324-8900

ESCROW OFFICER

**PROFESSIONAL
PROFILE:**

* 10 years experience with thorough knowledge of the Escrow and Real Estate Industry.
* Success oriented with high energy and positive attitude.
* Highly organized with attention to detail and the ability to service several transactions simultaneously.
* Special talent for assessing client needs and gaining trust.
* Supervise employees with professionalism, diplomacy and tact.

**PROFESSIONAL
EXPERIENCE:**

1989-present

AMERICAN TITLE COMPANY, Toluca Lake, CA
Vice President/Escrow Department Manager
* In charge of escrows for the main office and one branch office, working closely with lending institutions nationwide.
* Process millions of dollars in all types of escrows: exchange...residential...refinance...loan escrows...mobile homes
* Set up and deliver seminars and presentations for real estate offices in the San Fernando Valley area.
* Guest speaker for San Fernando Valley real estate offices.
* Hire, train and supervise a staff of 15 employees.
* Conduct motivational meetings for all staff members.
* Brought in a high volume of business through word-of-mouth, thorough industry knowledge and a large personal client base.

1980-1988

SAN DIEGO TITLE COMPANY, San Diego, CA
Escrow Officer/Foreclosure Officer
* Key member in the conversion of manual office systems to computerized escrow office procedures.
* Processed all foreclosures, maintaining strict deadline schedules on a daily basis.
* Handled large volumes of all types of escrows throughout San Diego County.
* Developed and maintained a large personal customer base.

1979-1980

SAN DIEGO BANK & TRUST, San Diego, CA
Escrow Assistant
* Assisted the escrow officer in processing escrows at this busy main office.

Winter-Fall '79

LAKE TAHOE TITLE COMPANY, Lake Tahoe, NV
Escrow Secretary
* Assisted the escrow assistant and escrow officer in processing escrows.
* Gained valuable knowledge and skills through company seminars and on-the-job training.

WENDY MACGREGOR
27900 Roseridge Lane
Montecito, CA 93108
(805) 684-1669

Objective: Position in Telemarketing Sales

EXPERIENCE:

1988-present

SALES SUPPORT/CUSTOMER SERVICE
Amvox Incorporated, Carpinteria, CA
* Develop marketing strategies, train, support field representatives for this manufacturer and distributor of voicemail systems.
* Administer 100 retail accounts with Kinkos, PakMail and Mailbox.
* Train management and staff; implement retail sales procedures and documentation, assuring smooth flow of business operations from installation through orientation of new customers.
* Resolve customer problems of technical and billing concerns in a timely manner to assure continued customer satisfaction.

1986-88

SENIOR ACCOUNT REPRESENTATIVE
Mini-Systems Associates, Santa Barbara, CA
* In charge of Colorado operations with major clients for this Aerospace Engineering Jobshop.
  - Honeywell...Rockwell Int'l...Contel Spacecom...Ford Aerospace Martin Marietta...numerous electronics manufacturers.
* Negotiate contracts to supply technical labor, monitor government contracts and track project dates.
* Research department heads and project managers extensive networking activities to increase manager contacts.
* Determine staff needs, job descriptions and arrange interviews; negotiate engineer contracts and all contract administration.
* Review all incoming resumes, network with engineers to find best candidates, verify background and job placement including engineer pay negotiation and travel arrangements.

1984-86

LIFE & DISABILITY AGENT
California Casualty & Life Insurance Company, Santa Barbara, CA
* Generated leads in telemarketing sales; worked closely with clients from the school districts, fire, police and highway patrol departments, University of California, Santa Barbara County.
* Planned, coordinated and set up custom packages for retirement, life insurance, annuity and IRA contributions and investments.
* Delivered policies, maintained billing and continued efficient customer service of all accounts.
* Achieved highest premium sold, 9 out of 16 months.

1981-84

OWNER, Dery Farm Country Classics, Santa Barbara, CA
* Established a complete giftware line.
* Designed and managed all stages of manufacturing, packaging and shipping from raw material to finish product.
* Developed effective advertising and marketing campaigns.
* Designed and composed wholesale and retail catalogs.
* Developed a successful home show business for retail distribution; represented line in Los Angeles Trade Mart and exhibited product line, representing company at trade shows.

STACY L. O'BRIEN
164 West End Avenue
New York, NY 01023
(212) 332-5980

Objective: An Electrical Engineering position

PROFESSIONAL PROFILE:

* Experienced in electrical and civil engineering.
* Resourceful; skilled in analyzing and solving problems.
* Highly organized, dedicated with a positive mental attitude.
* Excellent written, oral and interpersonal communication skills.
* Problem solver/team player with proven leadership qualities.

EDUCATION:

BS Degree, Electrical Engineering, 1990
New York University, New York City, NY

EXPERIENCE:

1986-present

CITY OF NEW YORK, New York, NY
(Department of Public Works-Bureau of Street Lighting)
Electrical Engineering Assistant
* Prepare lighting system design in coordination with Cal-Trans, Bureau of Engineering and other agencies.
* Perform calculations, utilizing plans and material specifications.
* Determine locations for street lighting facilities.
* Meet with the public and employees of other agencies to discuss various aspects of design and operation.

CITY OF NEW YORK, New York, NY
(Department of Water and Power)
Electrical Engineering Assistant
* Worked in new business section concerning power distribution.
* Designed drawing specifications for customer power upgrade.

1984-85

LONG BEACH NAVAL SHIPYARD, Long Beach, CA
Electrical Engineering Trainee
* Analyzed power requirements and ensured the adequacy of power generation equipment.
* Designed the arrangement and installation of electrically operated machinery and equipment.
* Prepared drafting, layout and detailed design using manual drafting tools and CAD CAM computer system.
* Researched manuals and technical specifications.

1983-84

US NAVY, Port Hueneme, CA
(Naval Ship Weapon Systems Engineering Station)
Electrical Engineering Trainee
* Observed simulation system and provided knowledge for design.
* Delivered and assisted in program installation on board Naval ships. Programmed computer weapon systems.
* Designed an interface unit for a more efficient computer system.

DEIRDRE A. LYNDS

671 Laurel Lane
Montecito, CA 93108
(805) 687-4567

Objective: Graphics Production position

EXPERIENCE:

1986-1990

COPY EDITOR, <u>Daily Nexus Newspaper</u>, UC Santa Barbara
Began as an Assistant Editor and was promoted to Editor through dedication, long hours, weekend work and the ability to work under constant deadlines. Edit all stories for news, editorial, sports, feature, arts and others. Position required strong writing organization and style skills, as well as faultless grammar, spelling and knowledge of style conventions of the Associated Press. Hire, train, supervise and direct copyreading staff.

** Won Recognition of Editorial Contribution Award, 1988

GRAPHICS/PRODUCTION. Responsible for daily assembly of entire paper. Required precision and versatility with graphics equipment as well as graphic creativity. Ability to read design layout; knowledge of pica and columnar measuring systems, point sizes, typefaces, half-tone/line shot techniques and equipment.

** Achieved Most Outstanding Production Staff Member, 1987

1985-86

PROOFER/TYPESETTER/PRODUCTION, <u>Goleta Sun</u>, Goleta, CA
Proofread entire paper. Edited opinion columns, news service material, operated extensive computer typesetting and paste-up of all corrections. Developed in-depth familiarity with specific guidelines associated with editing of opinion material.

Winter-Fall 1985

CUSTOMER SERVICE/SALES/A/R, <u>Hydrex Pest Control</u>, Goleta, CA
Held dual position, with responsibility for busy phone sales/service in addition to handling collections on all delinquent accounts. Extensive file research was required to obtain collection information. Developed excellent interpersonal/public relations skills.

<u>**Relevant Skills**</u>
* Computer - Compugraphic, WordStar, MacIntosh
* 10-key by touch
* Multi-line phones
* Scheduling/Dispatching
* Typesetting

EDUCATION:

BA Degree, Music Composition
<u>University of California</u>, Santa Barbara
Graduated: December 1988   GPA: 3.64
Dean's Honor List for Scholastic Excellence

OUTSIDE ACTIVITIES:

Active in organizing performances of original compositions and classical guitar.

LAURA ANN NEW
335 Rocky Creek Road
Boise, ID, 83712
(208) 342-9990

Lieutenant Colonel
Idaho Air National Guard
125th USAF Clinic, Riverton, ID

OBJECTIVE:	A Civilian Nursing position in a US Military <u>Health Care Facility</u>
LICENSE/ EDUCATION:	**BS Degree - Nursing,** 1973 - Summa Cum Laude <u>Idaho State University</u>, Boise, ID **Registered Nurse,** <u>State of Idaho</u> (A123456) State of Idaho Standard Lifetime Services Credential
MILITARY TRAINING:	* Advanced Nursing Service Management, 1986 * Nursing Service Management for Air Reserve Forces, 1985 * Air Command and Staff College, 1982 * Regular attendance, Association of Military Surgeons of the US * Regular attendance, annual active duty, USAF hospitals in the Western United States.

EXPERIENCE:

1986-present

CLINICAL NURSE (RN), <u>County of Boise</u>, Health Care Services, Boise, ID. Provide health care services at this very busy clinic of 18,000 patients (annually) in numerous clinics throughout the facility: Family Planning, Tuberculosis screening and referral, Well Baby Clinics (CHDP), Immunizations, Pregnancy Testing, counseling and referral, Primary Care, <u>total</u> Obstetrical Outpatient care, Blood Pressure screening. Operate clinical laboratory, ordering and maintaining supplies, compiling statistics, supervision of service aides, traige, crisis intervention including psychiatric, social/medical referral, pre/post HIV counseling, supervise and monitor patient care and follow up. Knowledgeable and capable of communicating with patients in Spanish.

1975-76

SCHOOL NURSE (PHN), <u>Boise Colony School District</u>, Boise, ID. Provided comprehensive health care services for 600 students grade K-8 in a low socioeconomic area. Extensive parent/ student health care counseling experience. Revised health services program to qualify for Title I funding.

1974-75

MIGRANT NURSE (PHN), <u>Boise County Department of Education Migrant Education Program</u>, Boise, ID. Traveled extensively throughout the valley area to provide health care services, physical exams, referral and follow-up care to children qualifying under Migrant Services and AFDC funding. Developed working knowledge of Spanish.

AFFILIATIONS:

* Association of Medical Surgeons of the United States
* Air National Guard Association
* ANG Nurses Association

39804 Oceanana Place
Manhattan Beach, CA   90266
(213) 360-2250

===

Objective: A Finance Management/Marketing position

EDUCATION:

MBA Degree - Management, 1985
Golden Gate University, San Francisco, CA

BA Degree - Sociology
Miami University, Oxford, OH, 1971

QUALIFICATION SUMMARY:

16 years experience in the Investment and Finance Industries. Strong emphasis on operations and reorganizational skills with the ability to rapidly analyze and recognize problems and opportunities. Successfully market products, services and concepts maintaining excellent customer and employee relations, resulting in production and profitability in highly competitive markets.

EXPERIENCE:

1986-90

EXECUTIVE VICE PRESIDENT, American Pension Consultants Inc, Los Angeles, CA. Managed entire operations involving $800K annual sales, reporting directly to the Board of Directors. Successfully designed and implemented investment advisory service. Established collective trusts with local bank involving hiring portfolio managers nationwide. Utilized research and marketing skills to evaluate portfolio managers and select effective performance monitoring system for collective trusts.

1982-86

VICE PRESIDENT, Mary Selbert Inc, San Jose, CA. Provided computerized lease and real estate financial analysis on a time share basis working closely with commercial and investment bankers and brokers nationwide. Involved travel to major cities conducting presentations to market product strategies. Analyzed problem areas and successfully developed and implemented programs to improve operations. Increased sales from $2M to $6M, expanding its corporate staff and offices.

1977-82

VICE PRESIDENT, Bradford & Geary Co, San Francisco, CA. Responsible for equipment transactions worth up to $100M. Developed innovative marketing and placement strategies for this tax-leveraged leasing firm. Worked closely with investors, lessees, regional managers and sales representatives throughout the country. Trained and managed regional finance coordinators.

1972-77

PORTFOLIO MANAGER ASSISTANT, Louis & Co, San Francisco, CA. Liaison between investors, stockbrokers and bank officers. Researched and successfully solved problems for 30 portfolios; developed investment proposals and comparative performance data for presentations.

PAULINA CANTWELL
2905 Whittley Drive
Washington, DC   13201
(202) 234-1809

RETAIL SALES MANAGER

**PROFESSIONAL
OBJECTIVE:**

An innovative and progressive company in the <u>Fashion Industry</u>

**PROFESSIONAL
PROFILE:**

Success oriented with high energy and a positive mental attitude...strong sense of responsibility and self motivation...good written and oral communication skills...great problem solver and team leader/player abilities...highly creative, flexible and efficient work habits.

**QUALIFICATION
SUMMARY:**

Five years professional experience of proven leadership and salesability in the retail Fashion Industry. Emphasize strong sales techniques, excellent employee and customer relations, resulting in production and profitability in this highly competitive market. Responsible for over $1M annual sales and merchandise.

**PROFESSIONAL
EXPERIENCE:**

1984-90

SALES MANAGER, <u>Rumours</u>, Washington, DC. Started as a sales clerk for this busy medium sized fashion boutique. Responsible for entire retail sales operation, maintaining $100K monthly inventory for two locations. Hired, trained and supervised a dynamic staff of 20 personnel, maintaining excellent employee relations. Conducted motivational sales meetings for all staff.

Developed successful advertising campaigns for promotions and sales involving fashion shows, direct mailouts and trunk shows. Generated and maintained new business, successfully developing a large personal customer base and created and maintained a "Preferred Customer List" that included customer follow up. Position involved buying ($65K monthly), inventory and quality control, merchandising, shipping and receiving, accounts payable, payroll, banking and cash management.

** Consistently increased sales 25% over quota.

** Successfully reorganized entire department and rewrote employee training manual and new, effective policy and procedures.

** Converted manual accounting procedures to in-house computerized accounting system.

DIANE AMANDA WHITE
60 Valley Creek Road
Montecito, CA 93108
(805) 962-5044

MEDICAL SALES REPRESENTATIVE

PROFESSIONAL OBJECTIVE:

Seeking a progressive company in the medical field offering salary and commission sales with unlimited earning potential.

PROFESSIONAL PROFILE:

Success oriented with high energy and a positive mental attitude...strong sense of responsibility and self motivation...good written and oral communication skills...attention to detail...great problem solver and team player with the ability to work independently...ability to cultivate business relationships with people of various professional and personal backgrounds...creative... flexible and efficient.

EDUCATION:

BA Degree - Psychology/Sociology 1973
University of Oregon, Portland, OR

PROFESSIONAL EXPERIENCE:

1976-present

SR TERRITORY MANAGER/SALES REPRESENTATIVE
Stuart Laboratories, Santa Barbara, CA. Sell tube feeding equipment, feeding pumps and devises and infant and adult nutritional products to hospitals, nursing homes, physicians and public health clinics throughout the Santa Barbara to San Luis Obispo territory. Successful sale of product line required full use of the proven abilities to assess physician and patient needs and present appropriate products through the consultants approach. Sample and demonstrate products.

** Developed highest market share of pediatric nutritionals in the region.

** Maintained strong commitment to professionalism while concurrently functioning as Territorial Manager and Member of Pharmaceutical and Hospital Panels.

1974-76

MARKETING COORDINATOR
The Browne Corporation, Portland, OR. Provided product usage training for a line of urological and gynological instruments sold through trade show exhibition and telecommunications. Client prospect base included hospitals and physicians nationally. Monitored the smooth day-to-day servicing of all accounts. Liaison between corporate and field representative, maintaining excellent client and employee relations.

TINA A. BOLTON
420 Sandcastle Way
Provo, UT 84604
(801) 377-5620

SYSTEMS PROGRAMMER

PROFESSIONAL PROFILE:
* Highly organized, dedicated with a positive attitude.
* Strong analytical skills with attention to detail.
* Communicate well with clients and management in a highly professional and diplomatic manner.

EDUCATION:
BS Degree, Computer Science, 1980
Brigham Young University, Provo, UT

COMPUTER SKILLS:

* **Programming Languages** - "C", Assembly, COBAL, BASIC

* **Software,** - MS DOS, AOS/VS, DBMS, AOS, DBASE III, System II, UNIX, INFOS and Ctree.

* **Hardware/Mainframe,** - Data General Eclipse, C350, MV15000 and NOVA.

* **Hardware Micros** - IBM PC, IBM AT, 386 Based Computer, Apple II and Macintosh.

* **Hardware/Mini** - Jacquard J100, DG30 Desktop Generation.

PROFESSIONAL EXPERIENCE:

1981-90

REGISTRATION CONTROL SYSTEMS, Ventura, CA
Systems Programmer
* Wrote and maintained operating systems on Data General NOVA computers in Assembly language.
* Traveled to major tradeshows for service calls worldwide.
* Performed program definition and analysis, detailed flowcharting, coding and testing.
* Developed detailed user documentation and conducted user training program.
* Wrote a cross assembler for the NOVA Eclipse Series.
* Designed and wrote custom software packages in "C" language for sales lead collection, assorted report generations and database conversion programs.

CERTIFICATES:
AOS/VS Systems Programming, Registration Control Systems
Data General AOS Systems Manager, Registration Control Systems
Programming Jacquard Mini Computers, Jacquard Systems

ELIZABETH KIM
550 River Rock Road
Baton Rouge, LA   70809
(504) 227-9004

POLYMER CHEMIST

EXPERIENCE:

Coatings technology
Polyurethane based adhesives for composites
Silicone primers for aircraft transparencies
Aircraft transparencies
Polyurethane liners
Composite laminates
Laminate procedures

EMPLOYMENT HISTORY:

1987-present

STAFF CHEMIST
Southern Research & Development, Baton Rouge, LA
* Research and develop adhesion modification of the polycarbonate and composite aircraft transparency products.
* Evaluate suitability of polyarylates and polyestercarbonates as outer ply and structional materials in transparencies for high speed aircraft (ATF).

1985-87

CHEMESTRY TUTOR
San Antonio College, San Antonio, TX
* Tutored students in general and organic chemistry studies.

EDUCATION:

BS Degree, Chemistry, 1987
University of Texas, Austin, TX

INSTRUMENTATION:

G.C., A.A., I.R., H.P.L.C., U.V.

COMPUTER SKILLS:

Proficient in Lotus 1-2-3, Multimate and ChartMaster computer software programs.

REFERENCES AVAILABLE UPON REQUEST

DANA SIGLER
225 Woodridge Road
Montecito, CA 93108
(805) 685-4231

SALES/MARKETING REPRESENTATIVE

**PROFESSIONAL
OBJECTIVE:**

Seeking a progressive company with innovative products, salary and commission with unlimited earning potential.

**PROFESSIONAL
PROFILE:**

Success oriented with high energy and a positive attitude. Strong sense of responsibility and self motivation...outstanding talent for assessing client's needs...communicate effectively with all levels of management in a highly professional and diplomatic manner...great problem solver and team player with the ability to work independently...enthusiastic, creative and flexible.

**QUALIFICATION
SUMMARY:**

Six solid years professional experience of proven sales ability and management as "Top Producer" in the Sales Industry. Emphasize strong sales techniques, exceptional presentation and closing skills, and effective customer relations, resulting in production and profitability in this highly competitive market.

SALES EXPERIENCE WITH PROVEN TRACK RECORD:

1989-present

ACCOUNT EXECUTIVE
<u>Call America Business Communications</u>, Santa Barbara, CA. Sell a wide range of long distance services to commercial accounts throughout Santa Barbara County. Demonstrate effective cold calling, appointment setting and follow up. Deliver dynamic product presentations and write effective proposals. Identify clients' needs, problems and solutions through long distance analysis. Became #1 sales representative in the first year of employment through assertive sales ability, thorough product knowledge and consistent follow up.

1987-89

COMMODITY BROKER (AP)
<u>West Coast Commodities Corporation</u>, Santa Barbara, CA. Directly involved in buying and selling commodities, specializing in options. Maintain existing equity and client contact. Emphasis on telemarketing sales to raise equity for existing book. Develop and instruct sales training programs monitoring weekly motivational meetings for sales staff.

1985-87

COMMODITY BROKER (AP)
<u>Option America</u>, Santa Barbara, CA. Account executive for full service brokerage (FCM). Worked with as many as 150 clients, traded options and futures contracts. Emphasis on sales.

ANGELA NORWOOD PHOTOGRAPHY
5160 Denny Avenue #22
North Hollywood, CA 91601
(818) 762-2814

COMMERCIAL PHOTOGRAPHER

EDUCATION:

BA, Commercial Illustration, February 1989
Brooks Institute of Photography, Santa Barbara, CA
GPA: 3.85 Honor Roll/President's Honor Roll 7 times
Won "Pentax Tokina Photographic Scholarship" for $1,000
Won "Illustration Department Award" for outstanding achievement

BA, Business Administration, May 1983
Spring Hill College, Mobile, AL

PHOTOGRAPHIC SKILLS:

* Experience with 35mm, 2-1/4, 4x5 and 8x10 cameras.

* Professionally capable of lighting with Balcar, Comet, Norman and Speedotron strobes.

* Extensive knowledge of printing and processing color, black & white, kodalith and flat art copy films

CLIENTS/ PROJECTS:

Western Studios - Photographed production stills of Uncle Ben's Rice food commercial for company portfolio. Winter 1989

Half Baked Gourmet - Photographed and illustrated a food container with complete gourmet dinner for an advertisement and promotional display. Fall 1988

Alabama New Potatoes - Photographed and illustrated a sack of potatoes with company logo for farmer in Mobile, AL. July 1988

Photographer/Coordinator - Developed conceptual idea for a behind the scenes look at the filmmaking of The Long EZ; a two projector audio/ visual slide show at Brooks Institute. Produced, directed, photographed and programmed the entire project. Summer 1988

Internship, Henry Bjoin, Los Angeles, CA. Assisted photographer in filming commercial food products for Coca Cola, Cantadina, Kerr Pie Filling and Carnation. Gained extensive experience working in a professional commercial studio. Fall 1988

EMPLOYMENT:

Freelance Assistant Photographer for Art Pasquali, David Spellman, Carin Krasner, Daniel Morduchowicz.

Facility Coordinator, Brooks Institute of Photography. Studio Manager Illustration Department. Responsible for checking in/out equipment, scheduling studio space, assisting student using equipment and equipment repair. 1987-89

LESLIE ANNE LEONE

1265 Cedar Place
Los Angeles, CA 90024
(213) 344-2359

Objective: A Social Service Management position

EDUCATION: BA Degree, Sociology, December 1988
University of California, Santa Barbara

EXPERIENCE:

1988-present   BATTERED WOMEN'S SHELTER, Los Angeles, CA
Shelter Coordinator (7/89-present)
Hire, train, schedule and supervise shelter personnel.
Ensure proper maintenance of client records and statistical
documentation as required for funding purposes. Interface
with community agencies to increase awareness of agency
services and to promote services for battered women.
Demonstrate poise and confidence with extensive public
speaking as shelter representative and educator of domes-
tic violence. Administer funds maintaining strict budget
requirements. Serve as liaison between Shelter and Board
of Directors by providing monthly written and oral reports. Write grant proposals and assist in fundraisers.

Client Advocate/Volunteer Coordinator (12/88-7/89)
Responded to crisis calls. Determined women's eligibility
for shelter residency. Assessed needs of women and
children; provided appropriate advocacy, referrals and
counseling to women and children. Represented agency
through public speaking for the community educational
program. Recruited volunteers and organized Volunteer
Training Program. Created and implemented fundraiser.

Fall 1988   RELIEF HOUSE, Santa Barbara, CA
House Relief Staff
Managed this home for homeless, single, pregnant women
and mothers with newborns. Co-facilitated group discus-
sions used for conflict resolutions between residents.
Provided information concerning pregnancy and made
appropriate referrals.

1987-88   ALLIANCE CHARITIES, Santa Barbara, CA
Social Work Intern
Explained available resources, programs and registration
procedures. Made referrals and performed advocacy for
homeless and low-income individuals and families. Developed and conducted art and play therapy group for
children. Collaborated with other interns in complete
organization of fundraiser for Relief House.

DEBORAH LOREN GRAMMACY
Attorney at Law
5068 La Crosse Road
San Raphael, CA 94903
(415) 457-4440

EDUCATION:

University of Kansas, J.D. 1979
Wichita State University, B.A. cum laude 1974

ADMITTED:

California
Kansas
Commonwealth of the Northern Mariana Islands
Guam
Federated States of Micronesia

PROFESSIONAL EXPERIENCE:

CAPITOLA U.S.A., San Francisco, California Jan. 1990-present
Corporate Counsel to U.S. subsidiary of a French parent corporation. Primary responsibilities include real estate acquisitions, sales and leases for all U.S. operations.

JAMESON & ASSOCIATES, San Francisco, California 1988-Dec. 89
Duties include handling all aspects of civil litigation with emphasis on litigation related to real estate and commercial transactions.

JOSEPHINE, LINDY & ASSOCIATES, Agana, Guam 1984-88
Represented Mobil Oil, Chase Manhattan Bank, R.J. Reynolds, Duty Free Shoppers Limited and other major Pacific-rim corporations in international business activities. Also engaged in commercial real estate transactions, legal research and writing and probate matters.

MASSOLINI, ROCKLYN & DALAMO, Agana, Guam 1983-84
Represented Exxon, Foremost, largest regional bank and other Pacific-rim corporations and government agencies. Responsibilities included commercial and general litigation, commercial transactions, drafting of opinions and memoranda of law for corporate clients. Designed office system for debt collection on behalf of established business clients.

GOVERNMENT OF THE PACIFIC ISLANDS, 1979-83
Saipan, Commonwealth of the Northern Mariana Islands
Assistant Attorney General for United Nations trust territory administered by the U.S. Department of the Interior. Rendered legal advice to Social Security and Environmental Protection Boards, Departments of Personnel and Health Services and College of Micronesia Board of Regents. Researched and prepared A.G. opinions. Created and supervised system for staff review of legislation recommended for executive approval or veto.

Chapter IX

COVER LETTER & THANK YOU
LETTER SAMPLES

About Cover Letters

A cover letter introduces you and your resume to the employer. Providing essential information not found in the resume, cover letters are needed whenever you mail your resume to an employer. They can be personalized or generalized, but are written specifically to go with the individual's resume. The cover letter accompanying your resume requires three paragraphs.

1. The first paragraph states why you are writing, that is, what position you're applying for and whether you saw an advertisement or heard about the position or company through a referral or simply by reputation.

2. The second paragraph is a brief summary stating why you feel qualified for the position. What makes you different? If adding the Professional Profile section in a resume will make an otherwise one-page resume into two pages, I'll use it in a cover letter instead. Never use it for both or repeat what is said in the resume.

3. The third paragraph is the closing statement saying where you can be reached and thanking the employer. See the following cover letter samples.

About Thank You Letters

A thank you letter is sent after you've had an interview for a position you're interested in. The thank you letter should be mailed the day of the interview; it should be brief and personalized. Follow this three-paragraph procedure:

1. In the opening paragraph simply thank the interviewer, re-emphasizing your interest in the position.

2. The second paragraph reminds the employer why you are a good candidate for the position. Try to remember something specific in the interview to be mentioned.

3. The closing paragraph again adds a thanks and states that you look forward to hearing from the interviewer.

It might seem unneccessary to send a thank-you letter so quickly after the interview, but doing so will reinforce in the interviewer's mind just how serious and enthusiastic you are about the position. And that very act can separate you from the other applicants, giving you the extra something that leads to your being hired.

ANNIE SUZANNE SILVA
1996 Mountain Drive
Los Angeles, CA   90068
(213) 360-8999

DEAR PERSONNEL COORDINATOR:

Challenge...opportunity...achievement! These are three strong ideals which have led me to your company. I am interested in applying for a Marketing Representative position with your firm. I would like to express a sincere interest in finding out more about becoming an integral part of your marketing team.

With several years experience in marketing and management, I am confident I will make a significant contribution to any firm. What makes me different from other applicants?

- The ability to identify clients' needs, problems and solutions.
- Delivery of exceptional presentation and closing skills; establish excellent rapport with clients and vendors.
- Self-motivated, dependable and outgoing with ability to supervise employees in a highly professional and diplomatic manner.
- Demonstrate poise and confidence while speaking in front of large and small groups of all levels of management and personnel.
- Gained valuable business and personal contact worldwide.

Enclosed is my resume which provides additional information about my experience and education. I may be reached at the addresses and phone numbers above. I will be glad to make myself available for an interview to discuss how my qualifications would be consistent with your needs. I sincerely appreciate your time and consideration.

Cordially,

Annie Suzanne Silva

Enclosure: resume

MANDY L. KLINE
2209 Oceanview Terrace
San Francisco, CA 96328
(415) 342-9000

DEAR PERSONNEL DIRECTOR:

I am writing in response to your advertisement for the Management position with your company, as my wife and I are relocating to the greater Minneapolis area where our family resides.

I have demonstrated a high degree of responsibility, creativity and enthusiasm in my work as General Manager for a high energy, restaurant & bar, Head Bartender and Regional Trainer for in Northern California. I am confident I will make a significant contribution to your company now, and an increasingly important one in years to come. What makes me different then other applicants?

- Setup of entire restaurants from the ground floor up for several locations.
- Ability to rapidly analyze and recognize company problems, opportunities and solutions.
- Developed highly successful company-wide incentive and training programs resulting in significant sales increases.
- Supervise employees and deal with customers with professionalism, diplomacy and tact.
- Maintain a positive attitude under pressured situations.

Enclosed is my resume which provides additional information about my experience and education. I will be in Minneapolis in April and will be available for an interviews at that time. I may be reached at the address and phone numbers above at your earliest convenience. Thank you for your time and consideration.

Sincerely,

Mandy L. Kline

Enclosure: resume

DARCY LUANNE MITCHELL
234 Woodridge Lane
Northridge, CA 91330
(818) 885-1234

November 14, 1990

Dear Investment Counseling Firm:

I am writing in response to your advertisement in the Wall Street Journal for the position of Trust Administrator in Los Angeles.

I have successfully managed over $750M in the short to intermediate area. With over 15 years experience working with living and probate accounts, I've demonstrated thorough industry knowledge and proven success in trust management. I'm confident I will make a significant contribution to your firm. I'm success oriented with high energy and a positive attitude. I'm highly organized and self motivated.

Enclosed is my resume which provides additional information about my experience. I will be glad to make myself available for an interview at your earliest convenience to discuss how my qualifications would be consistent with your needs. Thank you for your time and consideration.

Sincerely,

Darcy Luanne Mitchell

Enclosures: Resume

MARY LOU THOMPSON
1605 11th Street
Bellingham, WA 98225
(206) 676-0008

DEAR PERSONNEL DIRECTOR:

I am interested in applying for the position of Marketing Manager advertised in the Bellingham Herald on Sunday, November 1990.

My eagerness in pursuing a career in marketing and management will be executed with the utmost enthusiasm, due to the exceptional structure and quality of your management trainee program. What makes me different from other applicants?

- A successful record of diversified experience in advertising, marketing and management.
- An eager desire to learn and the willingness and determination to do what it takes to get the job done.
- I am a highly self-motivated person, dependable, outgoing and a quick learner.

I am confident I will make a significant contribution to your management team now, and an increasingly important one in years to come.

Enclosed is my resume which provides additional information about my education and experience. I may be reached at the address and phone number above and will gladly make myself available for interviews to discuss how my qualifications would be consistent with your needs.

Sincerely,

Mary Lou Thompson

Enclosure: resume

KATY ANN WOODS
2209 East 9th Street
Austin, TX 78701
(512) 476-0001

January 8, 1990

Executive Search Committee
Beverly Hills Fixed Income Corp
190 North Canon
Beverly Hills, CA 90210

Dear Executive Search Committee:

I appreciate you taking the time to speak to me on the phone last Friday. Susan at CRT has spoken very highly of you and your firm. I am relocating to the Los Angeles area and my goal is to find a challenging position with an established investment firm. I am looking for an opportunity to be part of a successful, dynamic and innovative team of investment professionals.

As a former Portfolio Manager/Trader with LA Fixed Income Management for over 9 years, I have demonstrated thorough industry knowledge and a proven record of success in all areas of portfolio management. I have experience trading in all market sectors and building undervalued bond portfolios. Being success oriented with a high energy level and positive attitude, I am confident I can make a significant contribution to your organization.

Enclosed is my resume which provides additional information. I would appreciate the opportunity to meet with you to further discuss how my qualifications could compliment your needs. I may be reached at the address and phone number above.

Thank you for your time and consideration.

Sincerely,

Katy Ann Woods

Enclosure: resume

MEGAN AMANDA O'MALLEY
369 Pacific Coast Highway
Malibu, CA 90265
(213) 971-4443

August 2, 1990

Executive Search Committee
333 South Grand Avenue
Los Angeles, CA 90071

Dear Executive Search Committee:

I'm very excited about the prospect of a seeking a new position in the financial marketplace. Thank you very much for speaking to me on the phone yesterday.

I feel I am in a unique situation, because I have never officially looked for a job before. I started working with LA Fixed Income Management during my junior year at UCLA in 1980. I grew up with the firm, starting with the responsibility for settlements, progressing to Assistant Trader, then to my current position of Portfolio Manager/Trader. With over nine years experience, I've demonstrated thorough industry knowledge and proven success in portfolio management. I'm confident I will make a significant contribution to any firm. I'm success oriented with high energy and a positive attitude. I'm highly organized, self motivated and willing to learn.

I have been very happy with my experience at STW, but feel for both professional and personal reasons, I'm ready to make a change. Although Santa Barbara is a beautiful city, I would like to relocate to Los Angeles to be in a more stimulating environment. I am a hard worker and open to all considerations in the financial field i.e., in-house management team, consulting firm, financial institution, or another investment counsel firm.

My current salary is $170K, however I am open to a wide range of income. Compensation while important, is not a major motivating factor to me. My goal is to make a change by 1990.

Enclosed is my resume along with a letter of recommendation from my current employer. I may be reached at my home address and phone number above. I will be glad to make myself available at your earliest convenience. I look forward to working with you in the near future.

Sincerely,

Megan Amanda O'Malley

CYNTHIA ANN TROY
101 27th Avenue
New York City, NY 01002
(212) 662-5500

October 15, 1990

Sandy Roberts
Marketing Director, Arts & Lectures
University of New York
New York, NY 01001

Dear Sandy:

I am most interested in the writer position at UNY Arts & Lectures.

For years at The Village Daily, I've been on the receiving end of your press releases, media kits, and brochures. Having made use of your information to highlight university events, I came to appreciate Arts & Lectures' accuracy, timeliness, and thoroughness. Like you and your staff, I know the demands of taking information, putting it into readable form, and getting it out to the public. What strongly appeals to me about the writing position is the range and stature of the events that Arts & Lectures brings to the university and the community. I believe my background dovetails quite nicely with the job's requirements. Below you will find a brief qualification summary:

- Experienced published writer, specializing in entertainment, arts and feature stories.
- Outstanding ability to communicate with all types of people.
- Strong skills in interviewing and developing rapport.
- Ability to handle multiple assignments in highly pressured situations and consistently meet tight deadline schedules.
- Gained valuable business and personal contact in the Santa Barbara media and entertainment community over the past 10 years.

Let me add, it would be a pleasure to be part of an organization that helps to enliven our area with such music, dance, lecture, and performance moments. Enclosed are my writing samples as well as a resume. I look forward to hearing from you. Thank you for your time and consideration.

Sincerely,

Cynthia Ann Troy

HOLLY L. BLAKE
2215 Oak Street
San Francisco, CA 94361
(415) 888-1177

September 21, 1990

Faculty Advisory Board
Box 1290
San Francisco, CA 94361

Dear Faculty Advisory Board:

I am writing in response to the elementary teaching position advertised in the San Francisco Chronicle dated Sunday, September 20, 1990.

My dedication and enthusiasm for teaching extends far beyond the classroom. I enjoy working with parents to help improve their children's education and I feel that involving the community in our educational system is important. I am confident I will make an excellent role model for your students and an important contribution to your staff.

Enclosed is my resume which provides additional information about my education and experience. I may be reached at the address and phone number above. I will be glad to make myself available for an interview at your earliest convenience to discuss how my qualifications would be consistent with your needs. Thank you for your time and consideration.

Sincerely,

Holly L. Blake

Enclosures

JUDY MELISSA O'MEGAN
39804 Oceanana Place
Manhattan Beach, CA   90266

(213) 360-2250

January 4, 1990

Search Committee
University of California
VC Institutional Advancement
Los Angeles, CA.   90024

Search Committee:

I am interested in applying for the position of Assistant Vice Chancellor, Public Relations.

I offer a strong educational background with proven success in leadership for long range strategic planning and the development of comprehensive marketing plans to increase company visibility and enhancement. I am confident I will make an important contribution to your staff now, and an increasingly important one in years to come. Below you will find a brief qualification summary.

- 10 years professional high level management experience.
- MBA degree in Management and BA degree in Sociology.
- Successfully designed marketing strategies and brochures along with complete marketing packets for new product development.
- Conducted company meetings to explain government policy and procedures and to determine client needs and implement effective solutions.
- Gained valuable business and personal contacts throughout the Los Angeles area.

Enclosed is my resume and application for your review. I may be reached at the address and phone number above. I will be glad to make myself available for an interview at your earliest convenience to discuss how my qualifications would be consistent with your needs. Thank you for your time and consideration.

Sincerely,

Judy Melissa O'Megan

Enclosure: Resume & Application

DIANE AMANDA WHITE
60 Valley Creek Road
Montecito, CA   93108
(805) 962-5044

July 15, 1990

Regional Manager
Suite 458
PO Box 9000
Carlsbad, CA   92008

Dear Regional Manager:

I am interested in applying for a Medical Sales Representative position and understand that your company is currently recruiting qualified employees with these skills.

I offer 14 years experience of proven salesability, marketing and management in the medical field. With strong sales techniques, exceptional presentation and closing skills and effective customer relations, I am confident I will make me an important contribution to your company now, and an increasingly important one in years to come. As requested, my currently base salary is 50K.

Enclosed is my resume which provides additional information about my education and experience. I would appreciate the opportunity to meet with you to discuss how my qualifications would be consistent with your needs.

Sincerely,

Diane Amanda White

Enclosure: Resume

JACQUELINE ANN FRANK
301 Victoria Court
Asheville, NC 28801
(704) 254-9992

DEAR PERSONNEL COORDINATOR:

I am interested in applying for the position of Flight Attendant and under-stand that your airline is currently hiring employees for this position.

My eagerness in pursuing a career as a flight attendant is motivated by the utmost enthusiasm, due to the exceptional structure and quality of your training program. I've gained valuable experience in customer service, sales, child care and public relations, I am confident I would be an asset to your organization. I am outgoing, people oriented, communicate well with others and take pride in being the best. I believe that giving the best service to passengers is the key to a successful career as a Flight Attendant.

Enclosed is my application and resume which provides additional information about my experience. I may be reached at the address and phone number above. I will be glad to make myself available for an interview to discuss how my qualifications would be consistent with your needs. Thank so much for your time and consideration.

Sincerely,

Jacqueline Ann Frank

Enclosure: application, resume

INEZ M. AYRES
7892 Forest Lane
Santa Barbara, CA 93105
(805) 966-9022

March 26, 1990

Personnel Board Advisory Committee
Santa Barbara City College
721 Cliff Drive
Santa Barbara, CA 93109-2394

Dear Advisory Committee:

I am applying for the position of Matriculation Counselor/Articulation Officer, Job No.: 03/90-25.

My qualifying credentials include Masters Degrees in Student Personnel Services/Counseling and Educational Administration/Supervision. During my tenure at the community college level as chairperson and faculty, I met regularly with prospective and enrolled students to provide academic advisement. The intent of our collaborative efforts was to....

- evaluate individual's status relative to entry and transfer requirements.
- clarify matriculation requirements.
- develop individualized short and long range educational plans.
- establish a personalized rapport with assigned student personnel.

On a voluntary basis, I made presentations at area high schools to acquaint the students, teachers and guidance counselors with the entry requirements of the Radiography Education Program. I also addressed the potential issues of career change, educational transferability and higher education.

I have enclosed the requested application materials. I am looking forward to a personal interview to discuss further how my educational qualifications and professional experiences are consistent with the departmental needs. I am confident that I will make a meaningful contribution as a member of the SBCC Counseling Department. Thank you in advance for your consideration.

Sincerely,

Inez M. Ayres

DENISE M. CARPENTER
570 Allison Drive
Santa Barbara, CA 93103
(805) 569-1110

PERSONNEL COORDINATOR:

I am interested in applying for a part-time position with a reputable law firm. Currently earning my JD degree from the Santa Barbara College of Law, I will be graduating in December 1990.

I have developed strong skills in legal writing and research through volunteer work and school projects. With my educational background, proven success in office and project management and desire to learn and excel, I am confident I will make a significant contribution to your staff.

Enclosed is my resume which provides additional information about my education and experience. I may be reached at the address and phone number above. I will be glad to make myself available for an interview at your earliest convenience to discuss how my qualifications would be consistent with your needs. Thank you for your time and consideration.

Sincerely,

Denise M. Carpenter

Enclosure: Resume

MARYL COOK
324 Central Park East
New York, NY 10038
(212) 799-4002

PERSONNEL DIRECTOR:

I will be relocating back to Florida where my family resides in the near future and I am interested in applying for the Communications Manager position. As I am aware of your excellent reputation and aggressive commitment to the communication's industry, I would like to express my <u>sincere</u> interest to be a part of your management staff.

My areas of expertise are research, writing and design, public relations and management. Given my thorough knowledge and proven success with internal and external communication leadership in the advertising/newspaper publication industry, I am confident I will make an important contribution to your staff now, and an increasingly important one in years to come.

Enclosed is my resume for your review. I may be reached at the address and phone number above. I will be glad to make myself available for an interview at your earliest convenience to discuss how my qualifications would be consistent with your needs. Thank you for your time and consideration.

Sincerely,

Maryl Cook

Enclosure: Resume

MADELINE A. HARVEY
6902 Emmons Road
Jackson, MI 49201
(517) 787-0000

July 14, 1990

Management Recruiters
University Professional Building
6000 East Ferry Blvd
Detroit, MI 48202

Dear Sir or Madam:

Thank you for spending so much time with me yesterday. I'm very excited about the prospect of seeking a new position in the financial marketplace. I now feel you have a good understanding of what I'm looking for.

With over nine years experience, I've demonstrated thorough industry knowledge and proven success in my field. I'm confident I will make a significant contribution to any firm.

If you need further information, please don't hesitate to give me a call. I look forward to working with you in the near future.

Sincerely,

Madeline A. Harvey

MADISON O'REILLY
809 West Street
Baton Rouge, LA 70803
(504) 388-2111

October 2, 1990

Personnel Recruiter
333 South Grand Avenue
Baton Rouge, LA 90803

Dear Personnel Recruiter,

Thank you so much for taking the time to meet with me last week. As requested, please find additional copies of my resume for your convenience.

I am interested in interviewing with the companies you mentioned last Thursday. I'm very excited about the prospect of seeking a new position with one of these firms.

I may be reached at the above home address and phone number. I will be glad to make myself available at any time. I look forward to working with you in the near future.

Sincerely,

Madison O'Reilly

Enclosure: Resume

Chapter X

JOB SEARCHING & INTERVIEWING

Successful Job Search Techniques

What is the best way to find a job? Follow the steps below:

1. Look in the Yellow Pages directory under the type of company or industry that interests you. (libraries carry phone directories for all major and many smaller cities.)

2. Bypass the personnel department as their function is to screen out potential employees, a negative screening process.

3. Contact the manager in charge of the department you're interested in working in directly. Why? Because you may have skills directly or indirectly related to the profession you're interested in that only the department manager would be aware of after talking with you. (I've learned this to be true in many cases through my own experiences.)

    a. Bypassing personnel can be tricky! A good receptionist will screen your call and direct you to the "appropriate" department. For your call that means PERSONNEL.

    b. Unfortunately, if the receptionist asks who you are and why you are calling, it may be essential that you provide another reason why you need to speak with the manager.

4. When you do get through, ask if there are any positions available and tell him/her that your resume is in the mail; send a cover letter and resume to the manager.

5. Wait three days and telephone your contact again. Ask if your resume was received; set up an appointment for an interview.

Many jobs are not advertised. The manager you talk to will be impressed that you thought to bypass personnel. It works quite effectively. Always look in the local Sunday classified ads to see <u>who</u> is advertising. Then follow the above procedure. You may find a position available that interests you.

Another great place to look for jobs is in trade journals at the public library. Large and medium-sized corporations located throughout the nation as well as smaller companies will advertise nationally in trade journals with employment opportunities in professions such as law, biology, journalism or the fashion industry. In fact, most professions have a trade journal magazine or newsletter. Ask your librarian for the name of the trade journal or newsletter that would cover your profession or field of interest.

FOR EXAMPLE: If you would like to work for a daily or weekly newspaper as a managing editor, reporter, editor, ad rep, graphic artist or production person, <u>Editor & Publisher</u> is the trade journal for the newspaper industry. In each weekly issue, you'll find many jobs listed from entry-level to high-level executive positions in the classified section at the back of the magazine.

How to Apply For a Job With the Airlines

Each airline receives over 500 applications a month. Because of this competition, it is absolutely necessary to follow each airline's specific up-to-date rules when applying for employment. Simply telephone information and ask for the specific airline's employment number. (Sometimes they will have an 800 number.) When you call, in many cases, you will hear a recording of employment opportunities along with the proper procedure to apply. Some airlines require you to first send a self-addressed, stamped envelope with a letter requesting an application. Then you'll mail a completed application, resume and cover letter. Some airlines even require you to send a check for $10 just to process your application. The airlines are very competitive and service-oriented. The key to getting an interview is to focus your resume and application on service, service and more service. They want to know what you can do for them, not what they can do for you.

Scenario: An Interview For a Banking Position

This is an experience I had while interviewing for a banking position many years ago. The interviewer asked me, "How did you feel about your first banking job?" I thought back to the first job, a file clerk in the trust department of a bank - not a very exciting position. But I responded, "I was 18 years old and felt good about being a file clerk because working for a bank is stable. I had job security." They were pleased with my response, which stressed the positive, and I did get hired.

Looking for job security is something most employers like to hear. It confirms in their minds that you really are planning to stay with the company for a decent amount of time. But most importantly it provides a bond that is mutually beneficial for both parties -- employer and employee.

Helpful Hints: Things to Know Before the Interview

Going on an interview can be both nerveracking and exciting. Here are some helpful hints to think about before going on the interview. Following these suggestions can greatly reduce your tension level.

1. Call your local Chamber of Commerce and ask for information about the company. In the interview, when you are asked if you know about the company, it is very impressive to mention various aspects of the business. A little bit of research can go a long way.

2. For out-of-town companies, check with the reference librarian of your library for more information about the firm.

3. Bring three or four resumes with you on the interview. You could be interviewed by one to three employers. Hand a resume to each interviewer and always keep one for yourself. Chances are the interviewer will use your resume to interview you, and this will make the experience go a lot smoother for everyone. It's permissable

to refer to your resume during the interview, though I suggest you try to memorize the main points of the resume beforehand.

4.   Always bring a pad of paper and pen to the interview. Ask questions about the job and take notes. You may want to jot down a few questions before you go on the interview. Also, remember to write the interviewer's name and title (with the correct spelling) on your note pad to address a thank you letter after the interview.

5.   Remember, think positive! Focus on your strengths. Talk about what you do have to offer, not what you don't. If you're applying for a position you do not have experience in, focus on enthusiasm and eagerness to learn. Do not to even think about your lack of experience. Enthusiasm is a great asset that employers notice. Sometimes the employer would rather train an enthusiastic employee with no experience than hire an experienced employee who lacks that quality.

6.   After the interview, immediately send a thank you letter to the potential employer.

List of References & Letters of Recommendation

Most employers will ask for three personal and/or business references. A "reference" is simply the listing of names, professional title, company they work for, company address and phone number of those who will give you a reference. Always let your contacts know prior to using their name as a reference that you plan to do so and make sure they will give you a GOOD one. It's usually unnecessary to mail references with your resume and cover letter unless requested. It is however, a good idea to bring them with you to the interview along with a letter of recommendation. A letter of recommendation is the letter written by a previous employer on the company stationery, highly recommending you for the position. If it doesn't, don't use it.

What to Wear on the Interview

Always dress up for an interview. Your appearance will be the interviewer's first impression of you. Wear a nice dress or skirt and blouse. Even if you know the company employees wear jeans on the job, you are not an employee, yet. You want to look businesslike and professional. Dressing up for the interview shows the employer you take your work seriously. Believe me, it will make a difference.

Executive Search Firms

Executive Search Firms, also known as executive recruiting or "headhunting" firms, are generally useful if you are seeking a job or position above the $40K level. These firms are retained by employers, and as such, never charge you, the applicant, a fee. What kind of positions do these firms generally "headhunt" for? Anything from college presidents, professors and basketball coaches to corporate middle to executive level management, scientists, fundraisers, hospital directors, you name it.

The firms act on a retainer. Usually, they structure a contract for a specified number of months in order to conduct a "search." They're paid for their time searching, whether they fill the position or not. Of course, if they do, they may earn a bonus.

A "headhunter" will probably be more beneficial to you if you are gainfully employed though interested in seeing what's available at other companies. In other words, you're better off being pursued than doing the pursuing. However, if your experience and income level warrant it, by all means contact one or two of these firms. They're always interested in adding to their database of quality leads.

Specialized Recruiting Firms

This group covers a wide middle range of positions. Generally, if you have specific industrial or technical experience, such as computer programming, hotel management, nursing, food preparation, accounting, sales, marketing, advertising, manufacturing or materials management, just to mention a few, you definitely should contact one to three of these firms. Even though some of them may use the words "executive" or "search" in their name, they work strictly on a contingency basis. That is, they're paid only if they fill the position.

Here's the key in working with a contingency agency. Select one or more that specialize in your field. They will have more of the appropriate contacts because they'll be marketing themselves to their clients (the employers) as "specialists" in XYZ personnel. But be careful. If they talk about charging <u>you</u> a fee, leave. The reputable recruiting agencies are paid 100 percent by client companies.

For further information and listings of Executive Search Firms contact your local librarian. I found valuable books with listings of 2000 executive search firms nationwide at the Reference Desk section of our public library.

Another great resource for those of you interested in specialized executive search firms is the National Job Campaigning Resource Center. They've got a wide assortment of directories, at least one of which should help you get started. Both contingency and non-contingency (those that work for a retainer) firms are cataloged.

The directories are classified by profession (accounting, computers, engineering, legal, health, just to name a few). By industry: for example, insurance, hotel/hospitality, defense, banking, etc. And by geographical location. Plus, they separate contingency from non-contingency firms. It doesn't matter if you're into pharmaceuticals, plastics, packaging, or personnel, chances are the Resource Center's got a directory to meet your needs. You can contact the Center by calling Kenneth J. Cole, Publisher at (904) 235-3733 for information or call the 24-hour order line at (800) 634-4548 or write to PO Box 9433 Panama City Beach, FL 32407.

Employment Agencies

If you work in a less specialized field, the employment agency may very well be of help. Who uses employment agencies? Clerical office workers, such as word processors, phototypesetters and receptionists; assembly, electrical, and manufacturing workers; hospital attendants and hotel personnel, to mention a few. Employment agencies offer permanent as well as temporary placement.

The agency offers permanent placement on a contingency basis and may charge you a percentage of its fee. This often amounts to anywhere from one-third to one-half of your first month's salary. The company makes up the difference. Some employment agencies will charge you the full fee which usually amounts to your first month's salary. This may seem a little unfair in that those who can least afford it pay a fee. But remember, your competition is going to be a lot greater.

Temporary placement not only gives you the opportunity to work in many different office environments but allows you the time to find a company you'd like to work for. Many employers who use temporary help often hire employees through such services.

Professional Job Changing Services

During the previous decade a new category of professional employment service emerged -- the job changing or outplacement firm. These firms, sometimes one-person shops, go by such classifications as career consultants or counselors, employment or outplacement consultants, management consultants, even career or management psychologists! And as such, they will differ widely in their services offered. Some will prepare resumes. Others will train you in effective interviewing techniques. Still others will offer personality and skills inventory testing. Some may even offer to make a few contacts for you. What you get will depend on the firm and how much you're willing to spend. Yes -- they will charge you, and probably dearly, for their time.

When, if ever, should you consider using one of these firms? Realistically, when you're ready to make a real career change. In other words, you've got business or professional experience, but not in the field you want to break into. Or maybe you're at a point in your career (like so many before you) where you don't know what it is you want to do with the rest of your life. In such an instance, the career or employment counselor could be of great help.

Incidentally, the term "outplacement" is one you should become familiar with. It refers to the practice of companies attempting to find alternative employment usually for middle- to upper-level management.

Trade and Professional Associations

Are you now in or ready to begin a career in a specialized field? Anything from hotel management, nursing, personnel, teaching, transportation, computers, library, animal training, to you-name-it? If you are, don't overlook the importance of joining one or more trade or professional associations. What value do such groups have?

First, information. These organizations often serve as clearinghouses for inside industry information. They also publish trade journals, "Who's Who" directories, notices of various conventions, and so forth. The information you'll gain makes this a smart way of keeping up with what's happening in your chosen field.

Second, people. Networking -- the art of letting people know who you are -- can often make the difference in getting the job you want or in making that upward career move. The more contacts you have, the more potential opportunities exist for career advancement. The adage that "it's not what you know but who you know" has some merit when job searching.

Again, the Reference Desk at your local library is a wonderful source for finding the professional association just for you. I've seen books at our local library that list thousands of associations nationwide.

If you're excited about your chosen field of endeavor and are open to relocating in the future for the right career opportunity, consider joining a professional association to help take you there.

ORDER INFORMATION

Distributed to the Trade by:

CAREER PRESS

62 Beverly Road

Hawthorne, NJ 07507

TOLL FREE ORDERING HOTLINE

1-(800)-CAREER-1

only $8.95

by Kim Marino

The Resume Guide For Women Of The '90s

The College Student's Resume Guide